THE ARMCHAIR INVESTOR

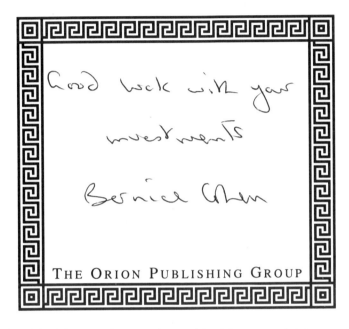

Good luck with your
investments

Bernice Cohen

THE ORION PUBLISHING GROUP

WARNING

BERNICE COHEN

···

THE ARMCHAIR INVESTOR

···

A Do-it yourself Guide for Amateur Investors

Cartoons by

ORION

First published in Great Britain in 1997 by
Orion Business
An imprint of Orion Books Ltd
Orion House, 5 Upper St Martin's Lane, London WC2H 9EA

A CIP catalogue record for this book is available
from the British Library

ISBN 0 75280 775 7

Typeset by Deltatype Ltd, Birkenhead, Merseyside
Printed in Great Britain by Butler & Tanner Co, Ltd.
Frome and London

For Amanda Davies of Fidelity Brokerage Services and
Richard Grant from *The Financial Mail on Sunday*.
They made the impossible possible.

Contents

Foreword

I first met Bernice Cohen a few years ago when she attended an investment seminar at which I was speaking. Since then we have met regularly.

Bernice is to be much admired for her intelligence, tenacity and drive, all of which have helped her to become an expert self-taught investor. In particular, her grasp of technical analysis now exceeds that of many professionals.

Many private investors feel that they would rather delegate the management of their investments to professional unit trust managers. This certainly reduces the risk of a major catastrophe, but it also limits the upside potential. Less than 10 per cent of unit trust managers beat the market on a regular basis.

By following Bernice Cohen's step-by-step advice in *The Armchair Investor* many private investors will be able to learn how to manage their own portfolios with confidence. With a few years' experience, they should be able to beat many of the professionals at their own game and beat the market on a regular basis.

Jim Slater
London, June 1996

Whose money is it anyway?

*Some of the most well trodden investment routes
lead nowhere.*

WHO NEEDS EXPERTS?

Woody Allen once described a stockbroker as someone who invested your money until it was all gone. Certainly, I had suspected for some time that other small investors, like myself, were probably none the richer after handing their financial affairs over to professional advisers. When I started my diary in *The Mail on Sunday* I began to get letters that confirmed my suspicions. Some readers had discovered as painfully as I once did that financial professionals are often no better and sometimes much worse than the rest of us at choosing successful investments. And if, by some horrible misfortune, they were to lose all your money for you, they would simply lose you as a client, leaving you to face the sickening Woody Allen outcome. When it comes to managing our own money, we owe it to ourselves to take more care than any expert. No one cares more about our money than we do ourselves.

*An expert is someone who carefully avoids making the
small errors while plunging in to the really big blunders.*

Once we realize that by devoting some time, effort and money to this enterprise we can do as well and most probably much better than the experts at making our money grow, half the battle against our earlier fears will have been won. The other half of that fight against fear will be conquered when we have learned how to pick the right shares to profit from our new-found expertise. Yet even with this strong incentive, most of us still secretly yearn to find a super-expert, somebody who knows more, somebody who knows better.

I certainly felt like that when I set out in the spring of 1990 to build a small portfolio of **unit trust** and **investment trust holdings** (terms printed in bold are explained in the Glossary on pages 193–6). These are the two chief forms of professionally managed collective funds available to UK investors. What I did not know at the time was that fewer than half the unit trusts actively managed by teams of highly paid professionals in the UK **growth and income sectors**, outperformed the **FT-SE-A All-Share index** in each of the last seven years. Even worse are the figures for the past five years, when only 28 out of the 206 funds beat the **index**.

The outcome is inescapable: small investors, like us, simply have to take control of our own financial destinies. At every turn, we have to make investment choices that might have a significant impact, for better or worse, on our financial well-being at some future date. And sadly it can take months, even years, to see clearly how well or badly these choices are doing. Great if we chose wisely; horrible if the choices turn out to have lost money.

BECOME YOUR OWN EXPERT

That is the bad news, but, on the bright side, the whole point of this book is to help you become your own financial advisor and make a success of it. When it comes to investing for your own future security, the buck really does stop with you. Even the decision to leave the money in a building society account is an active choice which may make all the difference to the size of your nest egg in future years. So it follows that the best, or worst advice you will ever get is almost bound to come from your own research alone.

THE DO-IT-YOURSELF ROUTE

The DIY bug shares many ideas with armchair investing: being handy and managing money are both useful skills. But we don't need to be professional builders or millionaires to recognize the advantages we'd gain. For both DIY and investing you must start with some basic ingredients – the resources that you have available. Just as your handyman gadgets can be fairly elementary, so can your investment utensils. Some of the simplest DIY routines produce exciting results; similarly you can create a simple portfolio that makes good profits but is reasonably easy to monitor. Just think, Warren Buffett, one of the most brilliant investors of this century, lives miles away from the major financial centres of America and does not even use a simple calculator to help decide which companies he will invest in. When both DIYers and armchair investors gain confidence and knowledge, they can branch out and tackle more demanding projects. As you get more experienced (and wealthy) as an investor, you may want to add some of the latest hi-tech gadgetry or devote more time to developing your new-found expertise.

If it was that easy, we would all be millionaires.

Whereas DIY jobs are seasonal and easier to do in the summer, investment is cyclical but the cycles are very irregular. DIY results may need watching, to be sure they remain sound. Armchair investors keep track of the cycles of the market and the economy, then respond to the ever-changing stories to stay ahead of the action. And of course, the great advantage armchair investors have over DIY handymen is that they can work smarter not harder, and achieve marvellous results, simply by following a proven profitable formula while sitting in their comfortable office at home.

Armchair investors and DIYers have most in common when it comes to the use of guidebooks. To improve your DIY skills you turn for inspiration to the manuals. They show you how to do things properly and expand on the range of jobs you can tackle. Similarly, for investing, many of the ideas and tips in this book are those that I have taken from reading books by or about the super successful investors. Many are American, but the ideas can be adapted for the UK market. As you read about investing, you will want to compile your own manual of those special routines that bring you excellent results.

Information is your most precious commodity.

This investor's guide is designed for those who want to take more direct control of their own financial affairs but have no idea how to begin to build up the much-needed confidence and skills to take the plunge. It is a step-by-step, hands-on-guide to the basic essentials of learning how to invest. I want to show you how to quickly improve your knowledge of the stock market and learn how to find and utilize the most useful financial statistics without being either awestruck or baffled by them. This will help you to build up your skills and confidence as an investor. I hope to take the mystery out of the market and get you started on the road to building your own stock market system. We shall cover the down-to-earth, no-nonsense guidelines that helped me to quadruple the size of my initial portfolio after my first six years of investing.

TWIN-TRACK ROUTES TO SUCCESS

Obviously, DIY investors must be willing to do some homework to make their investing successful. This may seem a burden, but do read on before deciding whether or not this approach will work for you, because in the following pages I will discuss two levels of interest. I will show you how to become a serious armchair investor from scratch, using one of my twin-track routes to profits. I will cater both for the all-out addict, like myself and for those more laid back amateurs who wish to run a profitable portfolio. I will show you how to achieve this successfully through proper monitoring without becoming a slave to it. This will prevent your efforts being overtaken by unexpected disasters while you spend some of your precious leisure time on other interests.

This is perfectly achievable in practise as I know from my own experience. For example, I developed my stock-picking routine, FASTER GAINS (discussed in depth in Chapter 2), during 1991 when I was still a raw recruit. By 1996, when I felt more confident with my stock-picking skills, I made less use of it than before, as I could rely more on experience.

Analysis using FASTER GAINS does take time to perform properly and it is important for novice investors to get to grips with the facts. Thus, because it has to be properly worked through I have never had the opportunity of explaining it in my *Mail on Sunday* diary, where space is at a very high premium.

When I set out to rebuild the family finances after spending more of our capital than was prudent on a self-publishing venture, I had not the faintest idea where to start. Learning from a state of abject ignorance is a painful and expensive test of nerves. During the autumn of 1990, while I was anxiously fretting over the impact Saddam Hussein's Kuwait invasion was having on my newly assembled portfolio, what wouldn't I have given to get my hands on a little plain speaking 'how-to guide', like this one. I didn't even know where to find the books I would need to read to discover what is what in investing.

By reading this guide I hope you will benefit in three ways: first, by making more of your own decisions; second, by reaping the biggest benefit when these are right and third, by having the courage and skills to change your decisions if they prove wrong.

PLUNGING IN

I have been a serious armchair investor now for six years. Investing in shares to build a sizeable nest egg is a long-term plan, especially if you want your money to double itself many times over. Six years is not long enough to know if my system will make me, or you, exceedingly rich. My results to date encourage me to think I have found a good formula that works consistently to give above-average results. I did not set out to make a million when I first became an active investor. All I hoped to achieve was to build up enough money to provide me and my husband with a comfortable and reasonably secure retirement.

Most new investors, myself included, are terrified at the outset by the thought of losing money by making costly mistakes. After all, if some experts have feet of clay, what hope is there for us to do any better? In this guidebook, I want to encourage other small investors to follow me by taking the plunge. I will explain my investment system giving examples to illustrate how I use it now. I will show you how you can easily modify my system to suit your individual needs. We will move through a set of simple steps to design and build a master plan with which you can run your own personal portfolio just as I run mine. This master plan gives a broad overview of where we are going and how we plan to get there. I am convinced that using a well thought-out system makes all the difference between success and loss. As the market is forever changing and my knowledge about it goes on growing, so naturally, my system has progressed from my initial state of almost total ignorance. However much I learn there is always more to know, but my success to date has greatly boosted my confidence.

I freely admit that watching the market has become a full-time obsession. My husband thinks I will never be able to 'retire' from armchair investing. But I am a great believer in setting goals and working steadily towards them, until they need updating. My goal now is to hold about 70 per cent of the portfolio in blue chip, long-term growth companies, like Reuters, Granada and British Aerospace, with 30 per cent invested in my favourite small growth companies. I hope to stop watching the market every day, and move from being an active armchair investor, to a laid-back amateur, spending more time on other leisure interests. I have grown my initial capital four times over, but I want to have grown it by six times when I make this switch. If it can happen to me, working slowly towards a better grasp of financial matters, it can be possible for anyone else who wants to make serious money from their investments.

Your investment system turns you into your own investment trust fund manager, in charge of making your own funds grow.

I hope that reading about my system will act as a springboard for many nervous small investors wanting to make the same giant leap into self-help investing that I have made. When my investment decisions go right, I experience a wonderful buzz, and when they go wrong I try to dissect what mistakes I made, to learn, if possible not to repeat them. And, apart from being rewarding financially, I have found Do-It-Myself investing is immensely exciting and a fun way of making money.

It is easier to make money than to keep it.
Anon.

CHAPTER 1

Method is not madness

*The trouble with learning from experience is that
the cost comes before the lesson.*

SHRINKING FUNDS

Right at the outset, you may wonder why you should start
investing in the **stock market**. Surely it is a high-risk area? In any
case, are company shares the best capital-building route? Money
on deposit in building societies, banks or fixed-interest investments
plays a part in financial planning, but it is the equivalent of
running on the spot. When inflation is higher than the rate of
interest paid, which has been the case in every decade (except the
1980s) since 1945, your savings are really shrinking as you hold
on to them!

Events could change in the future, but all the evidence shows
that over the past forty years or so, savings in deposits have lagged

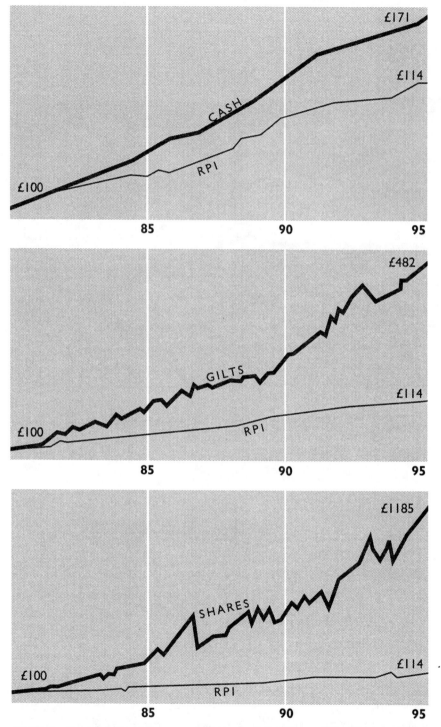

Figure 1 Savings over 15 years, cash on deposit, Gilts and Equities compared with the Retail Prices Index as a measure of inflation.

behind inflation, often by huge margins. When inflation is low, so also is building society interest, so the real growth in your savings will be tiny. With minute yearly additions, your initial nest egg will creep ahead at a snail's pace. Figure 1 compares how money grew over fifteen years, if held in the building society, **gilts** (bonds issued by the Government, which pay a fixed rate of interest) or ordinary shares (known as **equities**). The charts show widely differing growth rates against the rising inflation rate, with equities doing best. This has been the case in any period, long- or short-term, since 1910.

WHY SHARES ARE BEST

Equities are the real star turn for capital growth that beats inflation. Evidence from different financial sources shows that with good planning and the right know-how, the share-invested block of money produces a genuine nest egg. A yearly study by Barclays de Zoete Wedd, the brokerage firm, reveals the long-term returns from gilts and equities. Their records show that periods when bonds outperformed shares are rare exceptions. For example during the decade 1985–95, gilts, with gross income reinvested, returned 6.8 per cent a year on average, compared with 10 per cent from shares. An investment of £1,000 into equities in 1970 (as represented by the FT-SE-A All-Share index) would have grown to an astonishing £157,361 by early 1996, while in a building society deposit account, £1,000 over that same 26-year period would have risen to only £8,977.

Inflation spirits your money away without you ever knowing how this trick is done.

INVESTING FOR REAL GROWTH

American private investors put us in Britain to shame. The Investment Company Institute says that by year-end 1995, they had $2.8 trillion, or one-third of family wealth, invested in mutual funds (these are US collective funds, the equivalent to unit trusts in

Britain, which are explained in Chapter 2). This figure is forecast to rise to 40 per cent, where it stood from 1953 to 1965. Although shares often give the best inflation-beating performance, we cannot be sure that the future will be exactly like the past. But as there should always be new small growth companies coming to market, or shares recovering from a poor patch, actively investing on the stock market can bring success if you have a proper system for picking winners. And since we all face a big inflation cheat, we share similar investment needs. We all want a steadily rising income or a lump sum that grows faster than inflation.

For example, look at the record of M&G, the first UK company to introduce unit trusts (collective funds) for small investors, over half a century ago. M&G's free annual handbook gives many illustrations of how investments in their unit trust funds have beaten both inflation and building society savings over the long term (1950s), short term (1980s) and any term in between (1960s and 1970s).

Never give up on the market. The moment you do, it is sure to surge ahead without you.

Results like M&G's are not unique. Three equity income unit trusts (in which the managers invest in shares giving a high **dividend** to distribute to unit holders as income) appear in the top 20 performers over five years, even though they were competing against funds focused only on growth. In the five years from 1990 to 1995, Jupiters' Income Fund achieved an average annual return of nearly 27 per cent, turning an initial £1,000 into £3,292, Perpetual's High Income Trust turned £1,000 into £2,700, an annual average return of 22 per cent, and Credit Suisse High Income Portfolio turned £1,000 into £2,636, an annual average return of 21.4 per cent.

Although the level of risk is higher than with bonds, if your capital does not grow in the bonds you buy, inflation will be eroding it away even while you save. Real gains can improve retirement or provide cash to buy houses, trips around the world or other expensive items. But bear in mind, these unit trust figures are now history. Can they be repeated? And, more to the point, can you, working alone at home, ever hope to match this record?

Accepting that one will not always be right is an unpalatable truth that every investor has to face up to.

BUILD YOUR OWN WINNING SYSTEM

Learning how to pick shares need not be a tiresome full-time job. Once you know how to spot those with good growth prospects, you can be an active investor. Or you may prefer to hold your chosen shares for years, only selling if the growth halts or starts to decline, or when you find a better company to invest in.

Sadly, with investment decisions, you may not know for a year or more whether those you chose made money for you or not. If you are unlucky, you might have a loss. They may be excellent investments over a long term, but if they prove to be a poor choice, the task of recouping losses after a few years is harder than when you began. To avoid this, novice investors should follow their chosen investments diligently and change tack as soon as they feel uncomfortable with their progress.

Are we going to allow ourselves to become seriously poor, because inflation is always doing a disappearing act on our savings?

What I have found from trying to make money in the stock market is that for most people, investment success is not really a game of chance like roulette. It depends crucially on careful preparation. This puts you in the know, able to take key decisions as they crop up, to ensure success. And good preparation is built on an astute method. The method is your own personal, all-singing and dancing investment system. It covers your whole investment philosophy and it develops in two distinct stages. First, you must find a good stock-picking routine with which you feel comfortable, so you can decide which shares to buy. Once you have chosen a stock-picking routine to your liking, you must slot it into your overall investment scheme. This is the second big stage in building a system. It is a master plan through which you can design and run your own personal portfolio. You become your own fund manager, in charge of making your funds grow.

Your overall investment system is your blueprint for success.

WHY BOTHER WITH A SYSTEM?

Investment success depends on two elements. To make bumper profits, you must be invested in your chosen shares before the crowd joins in. When they start buying the share price rises, giving you your handsome gains long before they see profits. The problem is, anticipating share price rises before they actually occur is risky. They may never happen, or take many years to arrive. Hence the risk of losses. Even worse, the shares you buy, hoping they will soar, may suddenly collapse.

This brings us to the second priority. To stay ahead you must choose more winners than losers. It sounds simple, but I don't believe it can be done by chance or pure luck – it needs a system.

To succeed, you need only be right more often than you are wrong.

BEATING THE CROWD

So how do we beat the crowd, and make good profits? We must play the party game: pass the parcel. When the music stops, the chap left holding the parcel is out. Sadly, if you buy shares in the market as enthusiasm is rising, the chances are many Mr Know-all investors, who bought shares months before you, are patiently waiting for just this moment. They sell the shares they bought at lower prices to dawdling latecomers, including you. They bank their profits while you are left holding shares at the market peak. Evidence from unit trust sales shows that uninformed novice investors do exactly this at every **bull** market top. Unit trust sales figures for January 1996 show net sales (after redemptions) of £1.4 billion, the second highest figure on record. Yet during 1995 the **FT-SE 100 index** rose 20 per cent and many strategists predicted a poor year for 1996. Meanwhile, in February 1996, three major fund management companies, Schroders, Perpetual and M&G,

launched new investment trusts, raising large amounts of cash, although advisory **brokers** were cautious due to the poor timing.

Enthusiasm is infectious. Don't get sucked into buying investments after the market has risen strongly. You may be buying at the top.

If you do buy at the top, the next thing you know, the market is falling, taking your shares down in the general slide. And before you have time to think, you are sitting on a loss. This is such a bruising experience it stays with you for months – I know, because I fell for this idiot act a few times, in my early days.

Being ahead of the crowd by judging what they may do is critical for making big gains. And please don't think it can't be done, as the very fact that early investors sell out to the arriving crowd proves precisely that they achieved exactly what you hope to achieve. Simply stated, your main aim is to learn how to change bands. Give up membership of the naïve punters club and join the 'I-know-what-I'm-doing' brigade. The winners are patiently waiting to pass on highly valued shares to the Johnny-come-latelies.

When you have created your own unique investment system, work on it to improve your chances of success.

PICK MORE WINNERS

So here is the rub! To make bumper profits you must be ahead of the crowd. But to do this you must anticipate that your shares' prices will rise according to your plans. But suppose they don't? You risk losing money. A stock market cliché says the market climbs a wall of worry. But if you wait until all the bad news is known you will almost certainly be buying at the top of the market.

If you can get six choices right out of every ten, you should come out ahead. It sounds difficult, but it is far easier if you work with a good investment system. You can swing the odds more heavily in your favour by creating a made-to-measure investment system that fits your own special circumstances. Once you have created this wonderful tool, you can work on improving it, to increase your chances of success.

THE SYSTEMS APPROACH TO SUCCESS

So these are the chief purposes of your system: first, to reach your goals by staying ahead of the crowd; second, to be able to access properly the chances of profit versus loss. And third, to have contingency plans in place to handle situations that suddenly go wrong. Your investment system spans three areas to help you succeed: first, the broad outline – what are my financial goals? Second, the detailed plans – how am I going to achieve them? And third is the routine monitoring process – how can I ensure I stay on the right track?

You can swing the odds more heavily in your favour by creating your own made-to-measure investment system.

YOUR OUTLINE PLANS – MANY QUESTIONS

The first stage is to pinpoint the broad targets of your investment goals. Right at the outset, you must know what your investment needs are. Although in broad terms everyone would clearly like to enjoy a larger income and build a reassuring nest egg for the future, everyone has different individual circumstances depending on age, family commitments and life-styles. You must ask yourself a set of questions to reveal your unique goals. If you ask the right questions, the core of an investment strategy that suits you should emerge. At the start it may be incomplete, but the beauty of do-it-yourself investing is its learn-as-you-go, hands-on approach. This allows for continuing self-improvement, daily, weekly or monthly. The self-examination routine sketches out your resources and future plans simply by asking the following four key questions:

   i   Why am I investing?
   ii How much can I afford to invest?
   iii What is my money target?

iv   How big is my commitment?

Focus on these four questions to produce your unique 'wealth check', to identify your personal investment needs. The various choices between different kinds of investments can be a nasty minefield for new investors. It looks hopelessly confusing or off-putting. When you start from basic first principles, it becomes more straightforward. And the answers often lead to similar solutions. We all make broadly the same investment choices, regardless of age, sex or financial status, since everyone needs long-term protection through life assurance and cautious savings schemes, including pensions.

Money may not be the only key to happiness, but it can open up many doors that might otherwise stay shut.

SELF-EXAMINATION

Within the four big questions are others to flesh out the details. As you answer each question, your investment goals should appear. If your finances are complicated, spend time sorting them out. But try not to get bogged down. Stick to the broad outlines. Write down answers as you go through each set of questions, and decide your target goals. You may find questions I have left out, but which are important to you. The answers will be rough guesses, to be refined when your plans are up and running. This early process is simply to get you started.

   i   *Why am I investing?*
      (a) Do I need a nest egg?
      (b) What do I need a nest egg for? A family wedding? Do I want to buy a new house or car? Am I saving enough for my retirement?
      (c) How long have I got to build my fund?
      (d) How fast do I want it to grow?
      (e) Is there a financial deadline to meet?

A fool and his money are very fickle friends.

The same routine takes you through a group of questions if your top priority is to boost income from investments. For example,

       (a) Is a rising income more important than building capital?
       (b) How much extra income would I like?
       (c) Do I need it by a certain date?
       (d) How long will it take to reach my chosen level of income?

ii   *How much can I afford to invest?*
       (a) Have I any spare cash for regular monthly savings?
       (b) If there is spare cash, how should it be allocated?
       (c) Are my present arrangements for life assurance, pensions and regular savings adequate?
       (d) What do I need to do to find out if they are adequate?
       (e) Is there a lump sum of spare cash to invest in shares?

DO YOUR OWN 'WEALTH CHECK'

If any answers are unclear, do more analysis for your 'wealth check'. These are the central issues in sound financial planning. For future security, three areas – life assurance, **pensions** and regular savings – are the rock-solid foundation (your main financial wealth) on which to build your share portfolio. These are the essential building blocks before you start looking at shares. Everyone needs to pay proper attention to their financial fitness. The three main planks of life assurance, pensions and monthly saving schemes fit this bill exactly.

> *It doesn't make much sense to discover the value of money after it has all gone.*

Look at your savings and insurance plans. If you have dependent children, do you have enough insurance protection in case something happens to you, leaving them without adequate income provision? Are you saving monthly or annually into an insurance savings plan, a **PEP** or a **TESSA**? Personal Equity Plans (PEPs) are based on equities. All the dividends and **capital gains** earned within the plan are tax-free. TESSAs are savings accounts where no tax is paid on the interest earned. Both PEPs and TESSAs must be held through a recognized manager and the government has set ceilings on the amounts that can be invested each year. These tax free limits may be changed in future budgets.

If you are making regular contributions, roughly what increase in the sums involved do you expect to emerge within these saving schemes, over a five- or ten-year period? Do you make regular contributions to your pension plans? If you have a company pension scheme, will it give an adequate pension on retirement, or could there be a shortfall?

FIND THE CASH FOR INVESTING

The real meat in your money planning emerges by compiling two lists. First is the simple budgeting exercise, to see where your monthly money is coming from and where it is going. The second is a balance sheet of your possessions and debts. The bank calls these assets and liabilities. Whatever we call them, you must know what your full wealth check looks like. Working through the stages, some items may look incomplete. You can begin to remedy any glaring omissions.

Start with the essential items in your annual budget: income and money coming in, versus expenses and cash going out. Make a list and total up all your income sources, including bank interest. Now make a similar list of all your expenses. This will include food, mortgage or rent, heating, travel, entertainment, clothes, interest on outstanding loan repayments, hire purchase etc., and add them together.

By subtracting the total expenses from total income you should hopefully have a plus balance. It indicates roughly the size of your free cash pool for annual investing. If you find a minus figure, don't panic. You have just revealed why you can't pay your credit card debts. Or why the bank manager sends you expensive letters requesting you cover your excess overdraft. If you expose this nasty gap, try to plug it. Rework the expenses side of the budget to find some savings.

Don't spend what you haven't got.

THE ASSETS TEST

Now look at the assets picture. This is a similar exercise to checking the budget, but instead of subtracting yearly outgoings from income, you subtract your outstanding debts owed to others from your valuable financial possessions. List and sum together the values of all the big items. This will include your house (if it has been bought rather than rented), your car, jewellery, antiques, cash in the bank, PEPs, etc. Then list all outstanding debts and loans, including your mortgage and credit card debt. By deducting the total loans from your total real assets, you can see if you have a positive sum including cash, as a nest egg, or a negative sum, with more debts than assets.

> *It is a mistake to suppose that a man is a better man because he despises money.*   Anthony Trollope

JUDGING THE OUTCOME

The budget and balance sheet reveals your present financial state. If it is less favourable than you expected, ask yourself: what other cash can I find for investing? Which brings us to the third question:

  iii *What is my money target?*
      (a) How big do I want my fund to grow?
      (b) How long will it take me to reach my target?

Start with a realistic figure. I believe it is perfectly possible to double your initial capital over a period of five years. I achieved this goal in three and a half years, but after the 1990 setback there was a good **bull market** underway during the first two and a half years. Allowing a period of five years covers at least one (rising) bull and one (falling) **bear market** phase. And finally:

  iv *How big is my commitment?*

This may be governed by lack of time or even inclination.
    (a) Can I get reasonable results if my full-time job limits the amount of time I can devote to the necessary research?
    (b) Can I make good progress using short cuts?
    (c) What about all that paperwork?

Some answers to these questions will emerge once you start a trial run to see exactly what is involved. They are part of the action plan and will become clearer as you read on.

Saving is a very fine thing. Especially when your parents have done it for you.   *Winston Churchill*

DIVIDE YOUR SAVINGS

The next step is to organize the investment cash allocation. It is wise to split it up into several small blocks with only one for shares. Other blocks will cover pensions and insurance-based savings. Always keep some easy-access cash on deposit, for emergency events. Begin with all your initial capital earmarked for future saving in a bank or building society deposit account. Next, divide it into four smaller sections, each for a different scheme, to cover unit trusts and a main portfolio, plus PEP and TESSA plans where yearly additions will be made, pension plans and perhaps insurance-based savings plans, with cash on hand for regular annual premiums. The four sections therefore will be for (i) unit trusts and shares, (ii) PEPs and TESSAs, (iii) pensions and insurance-based savings plans and (iv) cash.

PEPs, TESSAs, pension plans and insurance-based savings usually start small and are increased in value by modest annual additions (plus interest or growth in the funds). Therefore, of the four separate funds two will start very small, and the cash and unit trusts/share portfolio funds will at first hold most of the allocated money.

From your big deposit fund each year, you will transfer cash into the smaller funds, so they are enlarging as the initial cash pool shrinks. If the investment plan works well, all the small pools will hopefully increase in value together. The key goal is eventually to produce a pension to provide a reasonable income in retirement, plus a substantial tax-free PEP or TESSA portfolio. Cautious investors can hold TESSA accounts for reassurance while they build the necessary expertise for choosing a successful share portfolio.

Don't rely on a crystal ball for stock-picking.
It may be cracked.

AN IDENTIKIT INVESTOR

The third stage in outline planning is to decide what kind of investor you will be. Have you a cautious or aggressive view of investing? Obviously, you are the only person who can answer this question, but learning from investment success stories of the 'greats' can help you find an investment style that suits you. Their books helped me to build an identikit picture of myself as a DIY investor. From the accounts I read of guru investors, I wrote brief notes on key items in their special techniques. These built up into a collection of highlights that were most important to me. Gradually, these notes crystallized into my core investment attitude. When I began, finding good investment books to read was almost as difficult as searching for good small growth companies. Now the gap has been filled by The Investors' Book Club, run by *Analyst* magazine, which offers a wide range of books, often at discount prices.

THE TACTICS OF YOUR PLAN

With focused ideas and rough targets, you can study how you will achieve them. This covers stock-picking, to find winning companies, and where to look for the most promising prospects. It includes market tracking, to make you aware of how **economic** and business **cycles** might affect your plans (cycles are discussed more fully in Chapter 6). It also tackles a vital topic, managing **risk**, so that you know when it is wise to hold a share and when it is more sensible to sell. These topics are discussed in later chapters.

THE ACTION PLAN

The monitoring process is the action plan of your new system. First, it includes good routines to monitor your portfolio and the market; second, it covers some organizational skills; and third, we will look at how to improve your performance, so you can reach your five- or ten-year growth targets. The action plan is covered in Chapter 7 and the plan in action is the topic of Chapter 9.

But without a doubt, a good method of how to pick stock market winners is really the meat and potatoes of your personalized investment system, so let's get started on that idea right away.

Save early, save often.

CHAPTER 2

Stock-picking to find winners

*Information is the cornerstone
of investment success.*

As William O'Neil suggests in his book *How to Make Money in Stocks* (see Appendix II, p. 198), and from my own experience, I have found that the best time to make big profits is in the first two years of a bull market when prices of most stocks are rising strongly. My favourite recipe for choosing winners is the mnemonic, FASTER GAINS. It is a formula for discovering small growth shares with king-size growth potentials and certainly works best in a bull market. Searching for **recovery shares** with the chance of substantial catch-up growth can also prove rewarding. But as both small company shares and recovery shares are risky investments, adequate preparation and research are important for minimizing the risk of losses.

THE FUNDAMENTAL ROUTE

A wide gap separates investors who study a company's fundamental data, called fundamentalists, and technical analysts, who rely mainly on technical information about the market and individual share prices. Fundamentalists often ignore the charts but I prefer *belt and braces*, using both fundamental and technical analysis to obtain as much information as I can from all the available sources.

Fundamental analysis relies on essential data relating to the current and future performance of a single company. A fundamentalist may also examine financial data for the national economy. This will affect the indices that cover its stock market. As part of the analysis, he checks the company's current share price to assess if it offers good value. Most fundamentalists use a set of rules for weighing up investment risks. The rules vary widely, but their use is a discipline to maximize profits and reduce losses. A good set of rules has helped some super-investors to achieve outstanding results, year after year.

Every step on the route to success has to be paid for, in time, effort or in hard cash.

TECHNICAL VIEWS OF THE MARKET

By contrast, technical analysts ignore the financial and factual data relating to a share or market. They study price movements on charts as they think the charts represent investors' collective behaviour. Charts show the total thinking of everyone involved with any one financial market or company. This includes market movers, like central bankers, analysts, brokers, politicians, and investors themselves. Within a price movement, technical analysts search for repeating patterns, hoping to predict how the price of a share or market will behave in the future.

Technical analysis covers many aspects of market information. It involves a methodical study of market behaviour itself, from charts, special indicators, and statistical calculations. This cluster of indirect information is used to analyse and interpret the past activities of all market operators, including speculators and long-term investors. But these active participants respond to influences from many background market movers, like the brokers or politicians. A range of technical data helps the analyst to decide if favourable patterns are emerging in order, hopefully, to profit from them. Technical analysts use this large range of indicators to make investment decisions instead of using the fundamental data itself.

CLUSTERS OF SIGNALS

Charts alone can give ambiguous signals. But confirmatory signals in several indicators together are more reliable; it is unwise to rely on one alone. When promising chart patterns appear, I search for other confirmatory signals. I use technical indicators and charts, but they are back-ups to the main fundamental story. I prefer not to buy a share with a super chart pattern if the fundamentals look doubtful. For example, during 1996 the price of British Biotechnology shares rose from 1,805p on 3 January to a high of 3,780p on 21 May, although the company is still in the middle stages of developing a cancer treatment which may or may not pass all the hurdles necessary for it to be commercially produced. Even in the early stages of the rise, when the chart looked promising, the underlying story was risky as the cancer treatment might fail the tests and never be marketed.

> *If you ride the bull to the peak, make sure you jump clear before the slaughter begins.*

STOCKING THE PORTFOLIO – INSTANT INVESTMENTS

Novice investors should tread cautiously while building experience to become proficient at their chosen stock-picking routine. For most beginners, the first stop for money earmarked for shares should be into collective funds. These are either unit trusts or investment trusts. Instead of buying shares directly, investors purchase units in a large fund. Millions of pounds will be pooled to buy shares in a wide range of companies. Therefore, your money goes into a much bigger selection of shares than your limited resources alone could buy, and this is a way of reducing the risk. The main difference between an investment trust and a unit trust is that an investment trust is a company of a fixed size that buys shares in other companies and is quoted on the stock market. A unit trust is not quoted on the stock market; it is managed by a company that prices the units in the trust and then buys and sells shares with money sent in by investors in the unit trust itself. It can grow bigger if more people invest, or smaller if they sell their units back to the mangers.

For the outright novice, even investment trusts are confusing, because they are quoted on the stock market. This means, at any time, the price of their shares depends on how much buying or selling occurs. Investment trust shares can sell at prices below (a discount) or above (a premium) the value of the total shares in the portfolio. If the portfolio's value is £100 million and there are 100 million shares which can be bought in the market at 80p, the trust is trading at a 20 per cent discount. If the same shares cost 120p the trust is selling at a 20 per cent premium. Trusts selling at a discount can potentially give good returns, as the price rises and the discount disappears, but learning how to judge which trusts to choose is a skill in itself.

After launch, new investment trusts that cannot generate much interest often fall to a discount. Investors wanting to redeem their shares will then not get back their full asset value. In early 1994, as the bull market peaked, two huge investment trusts, specializing in European privatizations, attracted over £1 billion between them at **flotation**. Both moved to an immediate large discount. The fund managers tried to reduce the discount but by early 1996, approximately 80,000 investors in these trusts had still not seen any rewards on their two-year investment.

The safety-first route is to invest in unit trusts in which unit prices relate directly to the value of the fund. In 1990, this is how I began; I chose a small portfolio of about three or four unit trusts. This is the cautious route everyone should use, until they gain more knowledge on investing. With such a wide choice of unit trust funds available, even this involves fund-picking, which can be just as difficult as stock-picking, unless you have a plan on how to set about it.

STARTING SMALL

Don't be deterred if you begin with just a modest sum. The famous American investor, Warren Buffett, had turned an initial $100 in 1956, into over $8.5 billion by the mid-1990s. Allocate a third of the cash earmarked for a share portfolio to buy three or four unit trusts (this will be one of the four small finds discussed previously). If you have £20,000 to invest in shares, one-third gives a trust portfolio of about £6,600, with £2,200 in each of three different unit trusts. Adding to these with a regular monthly savings plan, will build your holdings up more quickly to boost their overall growth when the market begins to rise.

PERFORMANCE MATTERS

Choosing three unit trusts to produce a good return after one or two years is an excellent test of skill in its own right, since there are over 1,600 UK-registered unit trusts investing around the world from which to pick. You can clip coupons in financial newspapers and send for information from some of the famous names in these funds; M&G, Fidelity, Perpetual, Save & Prosper, among many.

Bulls have herd instincts – first they stampede wildly in one direction and then in the other.

They will send a full package of brochures on their range of funds plus other details so you can judge their products. M&G, for example, will send their latest Year Book, with full performance tables of all their funds. The monthly magazine *Money Observer*, available by subscription, is helpful for comparing funds, as it gives performance figures for every quoted share, investment and unit trust in the market. Their tables show performances over many periods; for one and six months, and one, three and, where applicable, five or seven years.

DON'T BE MISLED

The do-it-yourself investor relies on performance tables for deciding which collective trust fund to buy. But tables can mislead, for example by suddenly highlighting a tiny investment trust with superb results. In a small trust, performance is boosted by one large gain, but it may be a one-off scoop. If minnows hit the top performance slots, investors should be wary. New money flooding into a hot favourite pushes the shares to a totally unjustified premium. Buying now will often disappoint new investors, which is why picking investment trusts requires skill. A tiny trust called Capital Gearing reveals the dangers. It was a unique fund, mainly privately owned, but its top place in the 1990 performance league tempted new investors, until it was trading at a premium of almost 100 per cent before it began to descend to normal levels.

A share may be rising nicely, until you buy it.

Always enquire into the reasons for out-performance when a trust hits the top spots. All trusts carry a 'health warning' that past performance is no guide to the future, and this applies in particular to specialized single country funds that buy shares in only one country. These funds are popular in newly emerging economies like Turkey, Eastern Europe and India. They promise large returns to investors. Such highly focused funds produce a switchback ride, mirroring the fortunes of the country they invest in. When they are in fashion they give big returns, as heavy buying boosts share prices, but they can just as quickly plunge down the league table in the following year, if they go out of favour and investors scramble to take their profits.

HOW TO CHOOSE

Checking regularly through unit trust performance tables is like watching football league results; different winners and losers crop up almost every month. So what does this tell us about our chances of picking profitable investments? It suggests that even the decision to trust your cash to professionally run funds can be a bit of a lottery. To avoid the flops, you'll need a reliable way of choosing which from the many on offer may actually make your money grow.

Beginners will sleep easier at night if they search for attractive funds which satisfy two main criteria. First, the funds should be large enough to spread their investments over a wide range of countries or sectors, to reduce the risk of huge price swings. Second, they should be trusts run by any of the best-known fund managers who have long, successful track records. Articles in the financial press offer insights into their investment attitudes. Searching among the leaders produces funds to satisfy even the most demanding investor. On 2 March 1996, for example, an item in *The Times* 'Weekend Money' quoted Jason Holland, an analyst with *Best Investment*, on the launch of three new investment trusts. He said, 'Schroders' [new fund] is going to be quite aggressively managed. It will only hold around 30 to 40 stocks. Schroders have a reputation for looking at hundreds and hundreds of companies before deciding which ones to pick.'

Money is not just a means to an end;
it is a means to many ends.

OPTIONS FOR INVESTORS WANTING LONG-TERM CHOICES

Armchair investors who dislike poring over tables to choose a unit trust can make a choice and happily stay with it. This will suit those who want a good growth record for a moderate effort. A well-established international fund, with globally invested assets, serves for the long term. You can switch into another fund whenever you decide a change may be more profitable. One way to reduce the risk of poor timing is to make regular small contributions into your trusts, even if the market is falling. When it starts to rise again, add a lump sum so your enlarged funds grow faster as the market rises.

START ON TRACK

Records show many professional fund managers have a poor

performance and do not even keep up with rising markets. The new range of tracker funds has emerged to avoid the lacklustre results from actively managed funds. Trackers have lower fee structures although these vary widely, as they simply choose a group of shares which represent those in the index they track. This reduces the costly time spent managing the fund.

A tracker fund aims to match the performance of the index it is linked to. The HSBC Footsie Fund, for example, tracks the FT-SE 100 index, which contains the biggest 100 blue chip British companies. Rising in line with an index seems a modest goal, but figures show few actively managed funds achieve even this. Virgin Direct commissioned research before launching its tracker fund in March 1995. This showed the majority of UK general funds, investing widely in UK companies, under-perform the FT-SE-A All-Share index, the nearest equivalent to these funds, which covers over approximately 900 UK quoted companies.

When you lose your money, you feel the pain.

Trackers are ideal for investors who lack the time or expertise to analyse the whole available range. If you can judge the market's main direction, discussed in Chapter 6, you may be better at picking a good time to start, when your research suggests the market may rise. If you just avoid investing at a peak, your tracker fund should make good profits. With this wide tracker choice, one of your first three unit trust funds should be a tracker. It is an ideal starting point for novice investors wanting to take the plunge into the stock market. But as there are over forty tracker funds, you must still compare the records as, surprisingly, some are far more successful than others.

GRADUATE ON SHARES

You might happily hold a unit trust portfolio for years. Monitor its progress regularly, at least once a month. In UK-based general unit trusts your money is invested in major UK companies. Begin buying shares yourself only when you feel confident. You can run your share portfolio in tandem with your unit trust portfolio, by slowly starting to invest the cash block you set aside for direct share holdings. If you began with £20,000, and spent £6,600 on unit trusts holdings, divide the remaining £13,400 into about five blocks of £2,680. With £20,000 fully invested, you will own five shares and three unit trust holdings. If you begin with £10,000 or less, I would stay with unit trusts until your funds have grown to around £15,000–£20,000 before investing directly in shares.

Although £2,680 per investment seems a small amount, this is no handicap. Many small companies with good growth prospects can only be bought in blocks of 500 or 1,000 shares. By starting modestly, the errors will be modest also. Although you may not make big profits if you begin with one small share holding, you can gradually progress. Increase the number of your holdings slowly, as your confidence grows, until you have added all the five direct share holdings into the portfolio. These will be chosen by whichever stock-picking routine you decide to try. Eventually, you might sell your unit trusts to buy other shares with the sale proceeds. I did this within two years.

The best boost to confidence comes from being right.

THE BELT AND BRACES APPROACH

We are now ready to take a closer look at my favourite stock-picking formula. I find making the right investment decisions can be extremely difficult, so I like FASTER GAINS because it includes fundamental and technical data. I call this my 'belt and braces' approach. It makes sense for small investors to study everything to get the broadest possible picture on what is going on.

FASTER GAINS is my tailor-made version of stock-picking guidelines recommended by William O'Neil, in his book *How to Make Money in Stocks*, based on his CAN SLIM formula. It includes extracts from Jim Slater's criteria for detecting mini-sized companies with mega-sized growth prospects. Jim Slater is Britain's most famous private investor. I discovered his investment approach in September 1990, in an article he wrote for *Analyst* (see reading list for details). I was so impressed by his ideas, I wrote notes on them.

Investment is subjective and rather imprecise, but FASTER GAINS covers the key elements for recognizing promising small companies. So let's begin by looking briefly at the typical profile of a FASTER GAINS company.

In the hard-nosed financial world,
borrowing good ideas is free to everyone.

THE FASTER GAINS PROFILE

To pick stock market winners, we must judge a company's prospects. The market sometimes ignores real value for years; although it may finally be recognized, this is by no means assured. We are looking for firms with big prospects before most investors discover them. We want to invest in strong growth companies with such attractive futures, other investors will decide to buy shortly after we do. So what makes a company valuable as an investment? Why will it be more valuable tomorrow than it is today? The answer lies in just two of its basic possessions: its assets and earnings.

Discover what makes a company share into
a fabulous buy and you will find that being in the know
is far easier than you suspected.

CHECK OUT THE FUNDAMENTALS

The assets are the actual physical valuables the company owns, like buildings and vehicles, plant and machinery, cash in the bank and its stock in progress. As a company grows wealthier, it can afford to buy more assets. The stock can be a valuable asset in its own right, because of its future potential. For example, early in the 1980s the pharmaceuticals company, Glaxo, produced a revolutionary new drug, Zantac, for people with severe indigestion and stomach ulcers. It proved such a block-buster remedy, revenues from Zantac turned Glaxo within one decade from a medium-sized pharmaceutical company into one of the most highly valued stocks on the list of UK publicly quoted companies.

The assets minus the company's debts or liabilities provide the positive figure at the bottom line of the balance sheet, called Shareholders' Funds. In an early recovery situation the assets might be less than the debts, creating a negative Shareholders' Funds balance. Of key importance to future performance is a company's ability to earn income from those assets. This magic ingredient propelled Glaxo to pole position in the UK market. Owning exciting income-producing assets is the mark of a growth share and the main agent driving fast-growing companies that go on expanding year after year. Buying shares in such a company is a bet it can earn even more money in the future on these important revenue-producing assets.

A FUTURE STREAM OF EARNINGS

A company's earnings decide the fate of its share price. If the price is high relative to the rate of earnings growth, a sudden setback may pull it down sharply. However, a company in a fashionable or fast-growing sector, like media, or in a new industry with immense growth potential, like mobile telecommunications or biotechnology, can have a high share price compared to *the rate of its earnings growth* as investors anticipate future earnings. As the earnings emerge, the high price falls relative to the company's expanding value.

> *Don't go sailing in choppy stock market waters without your 'belt and braces' life jacket.*

The share price related to its annual earnings per share is called the price/earnings ratio (PER). It shows how many years (in earnings for that share) is needed to recoup your initial investment. A share that costs 100p with a PER of 10 means it will make 10p earnings this year and take 10 years to cover the cost of buying one share. The earnings per share figure is closely watched because *it gives a vital clue on the future potential of the company*. The estimated *future earnings* is crucial here. So price/earnings ratios also look at how much earnings the current share price will buy *next year compared to this year.*

To calculate earnings per share (EPS) use the following formula:

EPS = Price of share ÷ Annual earnings on that share:

Example: Present share price = 750p,

Actual annual earnings per share (1996) = 50p

Estimated annual earnings per share (1997) = 75p

(Note: this is an estimated 50 per cent rise in the annual earnings)

PER for 1996 (current year i.e. historic) = 750 ÷ 50 = 15

PER for 1997 (next year i.e. prospective) = 750 ÷ 75 = 10

As you can see from the example, if the earnings grow by 50 per cent (clearly a pretty tall order), the PER will fall by 33 per cent (from 15 to 10). If this were to actually occur, by this time next year, the share price at 750p would be seen by the market as very cheap and it would be looking forward to rising 1998 earnings, perhaps of 90p. The market would anticipate the 1998 figure of 90p but if the share price stayed put at 750p, the prospective PER will have fallen to 8.3 (750 ÷ 90). This is almost half its 1996 PER of 15. To keep a PER of 15, the share price will rise to 1350p (1998 earnings of 90p × 15).

How will the market rate this growing earnings stream? Investors, especially in a bull market, might willingly pay 15 or more years' earnings to buy this share. This gives us two target share prices; one for 1997 and a second for 1998. Multiply the prospective 1997 earnings per share (75p) by the 15 years it will take the share price to recoup the 75p and you arrive at a first forecast target price of 1,125p (75p × 15 = 1,125p). If the price rose from 750p to 1,125p, the gain would be 375p per share, or 50 per cent. For 1998 the formula is (90p × 15 = 1,350p). Deduct the 750p current price of the share from the 1,350p and you might make a gain of 600p a share, or 80 per cent over the next two years, *always assuming the company can make this fabulous stream of earnings on its assets over this two year period.*

Novice investors need all the help they can get.

This calculation explains why small growth companies with a

wonderful range of widely demanded products or one block-buster idea, like Glaxo during the 1980s, are so highly sought after by investors. They willingly pay a high price to gain access to this future stream of earnings, especially if it is in a niche market with a unique product, or where there is little competition. Companies pay dividends out of their earnings, but many small, fast-growing companies pay only modest dividends to retain profits in the business to finance expansion or growth. The aim in buying shares in such companies is to enjoy the share price re-rating as the hoped-for earnings finally come through.

Companies, like investors, can get blown off course.

ROUTES TO EARNINGS GROWTH

Running companies is tricky; many unforeseen events at industry, national or international level can throw them seriously off course. Managing growth is one of the most difficult tasks they face. *For these reasons, investing in small growth shares is risky. Predictions of future earnings are unreliable.* There are, however, several ways earnings might be increased. A company can raise its product prices, expand into new markets or sell more of its products in its existing, established markets. For recovery shares, earnings rise when costs are reduced, especially if interest payments on huge debts are renegotiated. Here again, prices can be raised or loss-making operations closed down or sold off. For both growth and recovery companies, earnings increase if a new product is introduced or an older one is replaced. Very few companies manage to lift earnings each year by over 20 per cent. This eliminates most of the list you must search through if you aim to concentrate on this important criterion.

BENEFITS OF FASTER GAINS

FASTER GAINS is a means of finding attractively priced growth companies. It covers eleven factors. This means for any share you assess, you will explore eleven separate reasons for buying it.

Within this group of eleven, four cover the fundamental side of choosing shares, three cover the technical side and the other four are general pointers to help refine the selection process even further.

Given time, good investments make money
for you while bad ones simply stand still, or if you are
unlucky, show a loss.

FASTER GAINS therefore gives an even, broad-brush sweep, not weighted too heavily on either fundamental or technical factors. In essence, it captures my safety-first belt and braces approach. With its wide-ranging approach, it is ideally suited to investors who lack any previous expertise. It is the first weapon in your tool kit for identifying winners and avoiding losers; so it is another vital step for controlling risk.

Relying on several different reasons for stock-picking
is a sound way to hedge your bets against losses.

FASTER GAINS IN DETAIL

Although future earnings growth is a valuable element for appraising a company's prospects, it is certainly not the only one. FASTER GAINS covers the key items for unearthing promising small companies. Some are more important than others, but if they are listed in order of importance, we lose our useful mnemonic. So let's look now at what it stands for and then see, with examples, how FASTER GAINS helps to focus on those items I use for stock-picking for investment success.

F: Fundamental Facts. This is an overview factor covering all the fundamentals which give information on the present and prospective share prise. With the introduction of *Company REFS*, the monthly manual, it is much easier to judge a company's relative attractions as either a growth or an undervalued share. From the way the information is arranged, *Company REFS* quickly shows many key statistics, such as dividend yield, rate of growth, return on the capital employed (ROCE) and profit margins as a percentage of turnover. Black moons highlight the most favourable items. The more black moons on any one share, the more attractive it is as an investment, relative to others with fewer or no black moons. The vital fundamental facts you need for almost every share are given in *Investors Chronicle* soon after a company announces interim or annual results.

A: Annual Earnings Per Share (EPS). The latest annual results should preferably show growth of about 20 per cent or more. So few companies achieve this that this one item alone is an early weeding out process. With the current price and the future estimated earnings per share, the price/earnings ratio for this year, next year and two years ahead can be calculated. These calculations help you decide how cheap or dear the share is now in terms of its estimated future earnings growth. Target prices can be calculated, for one year ahead, as described earlier in the chapter. This important statistic (EPS) appears in *Investors Chronicle*, *Company REFS* and *The Estimate Directory*. It is the second fundamental factor in the group of eleven.

S: Supply/Demand factors governing the share price. A *small* market capitalization plus *strong* demand encourages a rising share price. Strong demand can also benefit the share price in large companies, especially if the market-makers are short of stock. This is a technical factor on the supply situation.

T: Technical Analysis. What clues does the share price chart offer? Charts help with buy and sell decisions, indicate target prices and trends for guidance on long-term prospects for a share. This second technical factor is fully discussed in Chapter 4.

E: Efficient Management can squeeze more profits from the same amount of turnover, increasing earnings per share, which helps a share price to rise. Efficient management is a general factor.

> *You are backing the management when*
> *you buy shares in a company.*

R: Rich in Cash. Companies which have no debt and handle products which generate a lot of cash can fund future growth without asking shareholders for more cash. When companies want more cash, they issue more shares. Unless there is a good reason to expect earnings to rise subsequently, the same amount of profit will now be spread among a larger number of shares, with a lower figure for earnings produced on each share. Rich in cash is another fundamental factor. It is preferable to have no debt.

G: Growth in Long-term Earnings Per Share. Growth should show at least a doubling over five years. The *Investors Chronicle* is one source for this vital long-term indicator, but from June 1996 the expanded version of *Company REFS* also includes this 5-year history of growth in EPS. It is another demanding fundamental test for analysing a company's performance. This doubling is so hard to achieve, it eliminates almost 80 per cent of the total list you have to search through. As it is such a demanding factor, it can be bent, slightly, but only if most other factors suggest the share is offering really exciting long-term growth potentials.

A: Active Monitoring is vitally important with small growth companies. Always consider selling on a profits warning, if there are unexpected setbacks or if the chart suddenly looks wrong. This is the second general factor. You can monitor a company's share price moves on paper, before you commit yourself to a purchase. How to set about this is discussed in Chapter 5.

I: Institutional Support. A little is good, but it is better if the main institutions decide to invest *after* you have acquired your stake in the company. When institutions buy, a share price often rises. They help to improve trading liquidity in shares. But to make 'super' profits you hope to beat the professionals by investing early before all the expected good news is in the share price. This is the third key technical factor.

N: Something New can cover new products, management or a new high in the share price. Similarly, N can be a niche market which confers a strong growth advantage. This is a general factor.

S: Stock Market Direction. It's heavy going trying to make money in falling markets. This is why tracking the market, to judge roughly where we are in the economic cycle, is an extremely useful skill for novices to acquire. This is the fourth general factor.

FASTER GAINS IN ACTION

Let's look at how FASTER GAINS worked for me in practice in 1995, with Medeva and Telspec.

To make bumper profits you have to be invested in your chosen shares before the crowd joins in.

MEDEVA FOR RAPID GROWTH

F: Fundamental Facts. Medeva is a medium-sized drugs company. It searches for late-stage, low-risk drugs to buy and then markets them. This differs from the standard approach, taking many drugs through expensive research and development stages, hoping one will be a block-buster. Medeva announced final 1994 results on 14 March 1995. The company was growing well again after a serious setback in 1993. *Company REFS* showed the growth rate, return on capital employed (ROCE) and profit margins were all in double figures. ROCE was 82 per cent.

A: The Latest Annual Earnings Per Share (EPS) for 1995 might be growing at about 20 per cent. For Medeva, EPS grew 24 per cent, from 11.8p (1993) to 14.6p (1994). If 1995 growth repeats 24 per cent, the prospective 1995 EPS is 18.1p. A modest price/earnings ratio of 15 gives a target price of about 272p (15 × 18.1p = 271.5p) for one year ahead.

S: Supply/Demand acting on the share price. Medeva is not a small company. Its market value exceeds £686 million. There are 286 million shares in issue. American investors hold around 17 per cent of these. American investors, plus directors and institutions together hold about 30 per cent, leaving 70 per cent of the shares free. This is a large quantity and is not a particularly favourable factor for Medeva as we shall see shortly, when we compare the figures for Telspec.

T: Technical Analysis proved extremely helpful for deciding when to buy Medeva. The share price chart is shown in Figure 2. I bought a small holding of Medeva in March 1995, when it broke out of a trading range at 187p. In August 1989 and during 1992, a price of 200p was a major resistance level (investors selling at this level outweighed investors buying, so the price could not get above 200p). In 1993, however, on three occasions, 200p was a support level (many investors buying at 200p supported the price above 200p). With this support, the price bounced up in January, February and April 1993. If Medeva broke above 200p in March 1995, it would give a very positive buy signal, as 200p might again act as a support level. This occurred on 22 March and I increased my holding at around 204p and 207p. On the sell side, 230p had been an important resistance level in November and December 1991, and in June and July 1993. Once the price shot up through 230p, it needed to hold above it (as earlier resistance then becomes support). In April 1995, when Medeva fell below 230p, I sold part of my holding.

E: Efficient Management. New managers came in to sort out Medeva's 1993 difficulties, when drugs approvals were held up by the American drugs authorities, due to problems at newly acquired subsidiaries. The chairman, Bernard Taylor, has extensive pharmaceuticals experience. He was chief executive for Glaxo before he joined Medeva's team.

R: Rich in Cash. At the time of its final 1994 results, Medeva had £9.6 million in cash, a very healthy balance sheet.

G: Growth in Earnings Per Share over the long term show how rapidly Medeva had grown. In 1990, EPS were 3.3p, in 1991, 8.0p, and for 1992, 12.3p. The fall to 11.8 in 1993 was a pause, as earnings per share grew to 14.6p in 1994. The 1990–4 rise was a huge 342 per cent.

A: Active Monitoring. This was important in Medeva's case, because shortly after I bought my holding in March 1995, they announced that another drugs company had been registered to produce their most profitable drug. This competition was bound to affect profits. In addition, in mid-April, Fisons announced they were in merger/takeover talks with Medeva. This attracted speculative interest, and it was harder to monitor the share price. Bid speculation pushes a price up rapidly, but it can drop like a lead weight, if the bid story unwinds.

To weigh the chances of success in your favour, try to ensure your investment attitude is in harmony with your system.

I: Institutional Support in Medeva's case was provided by strong American support. It increases liquidity for trading in the shares.

N: The New products for Medeva are its drug Methylphenidate, which is increasingly prescribed in the US for hyperactive children. This is the product in long-term danger from competitors. Another key product is Medeva's Hepatitis B vaccine, which chairman Bernard Taylor thinks will transform the group. It is to file for a licence late in 1996.

S: Stock Market Direction is the last, but by no means the least factor for making buy and sell decisions. In March 1995, the stock market began to ignore worries that had dogged share prices since February 1994. This proved a favourable background for investing.

I wanted to hold Medeva for at least one year, but events changed the story, as we saw. I sold my holding after two months, and made £3,764 profits on an outlay of £30,040 (12.5 per cent). For me, *this was a very large outlay*, but it was one of those rare occasions when there were two reasons to hope the share price would perform well. First, Medeva had excellent interim results; and second, the chart suggested once the price exceeded 200p it could stay above that level, as 200p would then be a floor, a support level. Like all small and moderately sized companies, Medeva needs active monitoring as periodically it has run into problems.

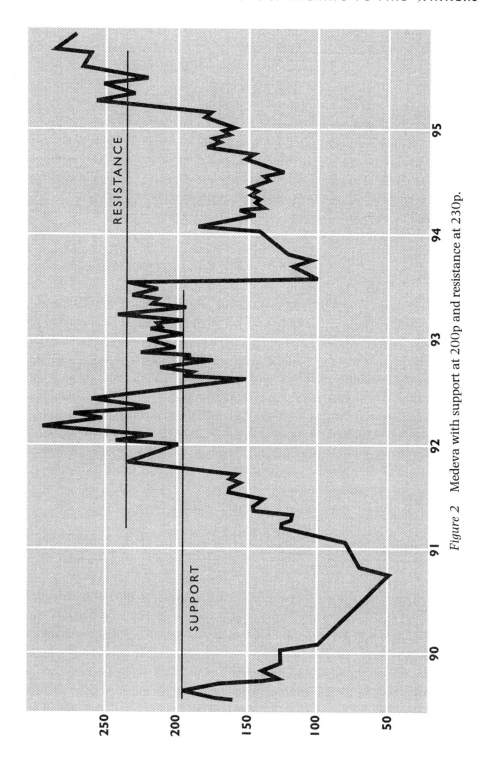

Figure 2 Medeva with support at 200p and resistance at 230p.

> *Stay flexible to avoid getting blown off course when*
> *the market does something unexpected.*

TELSPEC FOR LONG-TERM GROWTH

F: **Fundamental Facts on Telspec** suggest it is a growth stock still in the early stages of its development. Telspec supplies specialist telecommunications equipment, particularly for the telephone network industry. Its products are linked to the vast global telecommunications industry in which spending looks set to increase strongly for the foreseeable future. In *Company REFS* during 1995, its growth credentials stood out well and were all in double figures. The rate of growth was 45 per cent, which is so high it may not be sustainable. It was floated at 160p in November 1993, so its share price history as a public company is relatively short.

I finally bought Telspec shares at 457p, in May 1995. It had almost trebled from its issue price in only eighteen months. I hesitated when it was first floated, because I thought it relied too heavily on British Telecom. Sixty per cent of its business was with this customer.

A: Final results for 1994 were announced on 22 March 1995. They showed the latest **Annual EPS** were 74 per cent up on 1993, from 8.3p in 1993, to 14.4p in 1994. If the growth rate slows to 45 per cent for 1995, EPS for 1995 could reach 21p. At a prospective price-earnings ratio of 25, which is not excessive for a young growth stock, this gives a target price in one year's time of 525p (21p × 25 = 525). Further out, if growth continues at a more modest 25 per cent, EPS of 26.25p for 1996 could give a target price of 650p after two years.

S: **The Supply/Demand** factors for Telspec are very different from Medeva's. The directors hold 54 per cent of the shares; there are only 31.7 million shares in issue. This means just 36 per cent are freely traded. This helps to boost the price when many people are buying.

T: On the Technical Analysis side, even with a short share price history of only eighteen months, the chart on Figure 3 shows some key price levels. The first was at 290p, in February 1994. After a downward pause, 290p was reached again in June 1994. The next key price, 375p, occurred in January 1995. It was revisited again in late February and early March 1995. From there the share price rose to 500p with a slight pause at around 436p in mid-April, and by late September after the next interim results, the price soared to 775p. Both the rises above 290p and 375p were good buy signals, and then, another move above 500p indicated the next upward surge. We will study clues from chart patterns more closely in Chapter 4.

Buying information is your down-payment for making big profits in the market.

E: Efficient Management. Telspec's directors have large share-holdings. This gives them strong incentives to be successful. The chairman, Frank Hackett-Jones, holds 53.6 per cent of the issued share capital.

R: Rich in Cash for Telspec has to be modified slightly, as the 1994 year end showed a small net debt of 4 per cent. This is an acceptable level of debt in a young, fast-growing company.

G: Growth in EPS since 1990 shows a rise from 0.11p in 1990 to 1.23p in 1991, 7.13p in 1992, 8.28p in 1993 and 14.4p in 1994. The growth in earnings per share has risen 228 per cent since 1990.

A: Active Monitoring is essential for small, vigorously growing companies like Telspec. With rapid growth, events which interrupt the profit flow, like delays in supply of parts, order delays or other setbacks, quickly upset the share price. Managing rapid expansion is one of the most hazardous tasks for small companies. Early in 1995 and 1996, Telspec announced delays in sending out finished orders, which hit the share price. I do not think this is a long-term worry as Telspec's order book is worth £70 million, but it shows

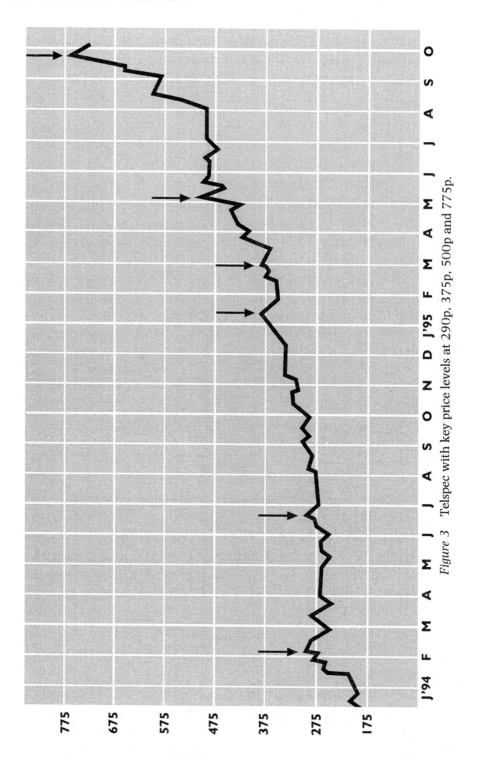

Figure 3   Telspec with key price levels at 290p, 375p, 500p and 775p.

that fast-growing companies must always be closely watched for upsetting news.

However much you learn, there is always more to know.

I: Institutional Support is currently minimal for Telspec, because the directors have very large holdings. In the future, perhaps, the directors might negotiate to sell part of their holdings directly to institutional buyers. This would be a positive move. The market value of Telspec at 720p is a modest £228.24 million (720p × 31.7m = £228.24m) and because the directors hold 54 per cent of the share capital, institutional investors have difficulty building up a sizeable holding.

N: Something New. The equipment Telspec makes ranks as 'new' products. These include a device for transmitting voice and text over the network, plus its most successful gadget, the concentrator, which turns one telephone line into two, thereby saving telecoms companies the trouble of fitting new lines when existing capacity runs out. Other important 'new items' for Telspec include new customers, reducing its heavy early dependence on British Telecom. It now has customers in Turkey, Argentina, South East Asia, Germany, Slovakia, Spain and Australia.

S: Stock Market Direction. During the spring and summer of 1995, the market moved strongly higher. This provided a very encouraging background for the share price rise of Telspec during 1995.

Don't give away big profits because you get impatient and can't sit with your shares.

I bought 2,260 shares for my PEP during May 1995 for a total outlay of £10,441 at an average cost of 462p. However, during the summer the technology sector in America seemed to be racing ahead too fast, and I decided to diversify into other technology shares, as I felt that having a large holding in only one small high-technology company held obvious risks for disappointment if things suddenly began to go wrong.

During August 1995 I sold 400 Telspec shares at 564p, and another 460 at 602p, for a profit on 860 shares of £1,020, a gain of 9.9 per cent in five months. I sold the 860 shares because I thought the shares were running ahead too fast. Yet, between 28 August and 22 September, the price shot up from 600p to 720p, mainly because Telspec announced extremely positive interim results on 5 September.

The share price began to rise shortly before, and again soon after, these good results were announced. There is often a period of six to eight weeks between the announcement of final results, the production of the annual report and the annual general meeting. These three events, coming so close together, often stimulate buying interest in small, fast-growing companies like Telspec.

The short-term risks in small aggressively growing shares were luridly exposed for Telspec early in 1996. Unfortunately, the positive chart picture began giving sell signals in December 1995 when the strong up-trend was broken. I ignored the sell signal, hoping it would soon correct itself. However, the sell signals were reinforced as a strong down-trend developed. Still reluctant, I finally sold my holding in two stages at prices of 770p and 735p in mid-March, around the time when Telspec announced its final results. The results were excellent, but the high share price left no room for disappointment, a view the market obviously shared, as the down-trend continued after the results announcement. On 8 May Telspec issued a profits warning and the share price plunged to 513p. This is a cautionary tale of how vigilant one must be when investing in small, rapidly growing growth companies.

THE ONES THAT GOT AWAY

Lacking confidence in the shares you choose with a good stock-picking routine can be costly, as I know from my own experience. During 1994 I sold out far too early in some selections with promising prospects that I unearthed using FASTER GAINS. I grew impatient with their slow progress, which is definitely an expensive fault. The ones that got away included Northamber, a small electronics distributor that I sold at 98p. Within a year it had reached 250p. Then I sold David Lloyd Leisure, the sports centre group, a few months before a takeover which valued it at 150p more than I got on selling. I sold European Colour, the small specialist chemicals group, at 67p, only to see it hit 100p within nine months.

> *The big profits come from riding up the lengthy growth curve as it unfolds for a small growth company.*

One big investment idea I had was to use FASTER GAINS to build up the value of a general PEP through large capital gains. I found this difficult in practice for most shares I chose. European Colour and David Lloyd Leisure were both PEP investments I chose well but was too impatient to let unfold. They were both excellent choices, and would have shown good profits, if I had been more confident about the outcomes I had originally expected. But I had two successes; one very early with Glaxo shares, which between September 1990 and January 1992 rose in my PEP from £12.50 to £18.00 a share (before a two-for-one share split). The second triumph was an investment in Unipalm, the small Internet provider. Unipalm was an example of a young, rapidly growing firm in a booming sector. The Internet was a buzz word in the early 1990s. Unipalm was making start-up losses, so profits fundamentals are useless for such a company. How I modify FASTER GAINS for considering an investment in young companies with no earnings is covered in chapter 4 on profitable clues from charts, using the Unipalm example. Chart patterns are very important in start-up companies for which future earnings can be only rough guesses.

> *Recovery shares are great, as long as they recover.*

RECOVERY SHARES WITH FASTER GAINS

A modified form of FASTER GAINS can also be applied to **recovery shares**, in which the fundamentals look cloudy but recovery offers attractive prospects. I use only the relevant parts of the formula to allow me to invest in companies with a promising recovery story. I check closely on the factors that are important for their return to profitability. For example, during 1995 I bought shares in WPP, the advertising group that fell on hard times during the early 1990s recession. Some pointers from FASTER GAINS alerted me to its possible future recovery.

Fundamental Facts were essentially unhelpful, as the company was making very small profits. However, as we noted on page 26, the crucial item to consider is **the future stream of earnings.**

Efficient Management. Analysts were positive about WPP's earnings recovery possibilities. Chief executive Martin Sorrell won the backing of institutional fund managers holding WPP shares, for a controversial remunerations package which would give him sizeable bonuses if WPP's profits revived. This was another positive factor for the company's future. Martin Sorrell stayed with WPP throughout its setback, but in other cases, bad performance forces out the managers responsible for it. The new team can be another good omen, if they implement different ideas for restoring the company's fortunes.

Rich in Cash. WPP's massive debts were a problem for me when deciding whether to invest in the company. I was not clear how rising cash flow would ever repay the debts, which were over £200 million.

Technical Analysis persuaded me I could make profits from a holding in WPP. The chart appearance gave a strong buy signal which will be discussed in Chapter 4 on profitable clues from charts.

I bought 3,800 WPP shares early in July 1995, but I held them for only four months. In that time the share price rose from 126p to 154p and I made a good profit. However, I was constantly unhappy about the massive debts, which is why I sold the holding. Then, in February 1996, the company's final 1995 results were encouraging, with a big leap of 33 per cent in pre-tax profits. Earnings per share grew 20 per cent, and prospects for repaying the debt looked far more promising. The chart again gave a buy signal and I thought the recovery would continue. I bought 2,000 shares at 189p but I was not upset by the profits I lost by not holding on from July 1995. I preferred to sell to reinvest after I was reassured WPP's large debts could be repaid.

It takes years to make an overnight success. Eddie Cantor

CHAPTER 3

Building blocks for stock-pickers

*You can't be right all the time, but you
sure can be wrong all the time.*

A trusty stock-picking system is an essential springboard for novice
investors but we still need a sieve to help spot suitable companies
that may qualify as FASTER GAINS candidates. We want to avoid
spending hours searching lists for promising companies. This
chapter is about how to unearth those companies on which we
want to use FASTER GAINS. Finding these little gems involves
three costs.

THE FIRST INVESTMENTS

Time is the first cost. Time spent on research can vary; like a piece
of string, it can be as long or short as you prefer. Successful

investing, like playing golf or the piano, can take many hours depending on your approach. If you know in advance how much time you can or want to commit, your schedules can be tailored to a timetable. Focusing on priorities can improve your results. It helps if you know roughly at the start how much time you can allocate. Then plan your campaign around that, making modifications later as necessary. The second cost is the effort involved in research. Here again, there are many short cuts, as we shall soon see. Success is possible with modest research efforts, if it is focused. You must grasp the main investment principles, devise your made-to-measure system, and then apply it.

The third cost is in hard-earned cash. Buying investment books, ordering monthly newsletters, getting real-time share prices into your home (that is, as prices actually change in the market), or using software to track share prices on charts, are all expensive investment aids. I never begrudge buying equipment, but it has to earn its keep. Periodically, I review the newsletters and journals I buy, to check if they are paying their way by alerting me to good companies. If I haven't found a company that interests me enough to do FASTER GAINS on after three issues, I close the subscription. It makes sense to have a trial run on expensive items, to assess their use for a while. I sometimes do this with books, borrowing from the library to decide if I would refer to it many times, and so want my own copy.

> *The cost of treasure hunting is measured in time,*
> *effort and buying some essential research tools.*

The best approach with investment aids is to start modestly; add more tools only when you see your investment strategy is working and the profits start arriving. If you can accept the outlay of time, effort and expense as your first investments on the road to success, you will not begrudge the costs, but will view them as the way to ensure you have the right tools to make a resounding success of all that follows.

RICH PICKINGS

Ferreting out companies with excellent prospects is the bedrock for successful investment planning. Time spent tracking them down can reap rich rewards. The best profits come from identifying small growth companies with expansion potential and holding them as they grow to maturity. Another route is to buy a recovery share once you feel confident all the horror stories of its fall from grace have been sorted out. The FASTER GAINS formula applies, but the debt position must be manageable. There will still be plenty of up-side in the share price when late arrivals jump in after you as the recovery story continues to unfold. A third area for making excellent gains is by buying companies at an early stage, where research and development costs outweigh current revenues, but there could be huge potentials if the new products they are researching finally attract large sales. These are often called 'blue sky' shares. They may prove wonderfully successful, but could equally turn into disaster zones.

Face up to the fear of making losses
by getting to know the facts.

All three routes to profits – small growth, recovery and blue sky shares – are highly risky, so thorough research is necessary before you decide to buy. But unearthing suitable little gems need not be time consuming or heavy going once you have a properly thought-out plan of campaign; with my investment style, you can become an armchair detective to sort out the companies with the best growth potentials.

BASIC COMPANY INFORMATION

Information is the cornerstone to success. But you must know where to find it, how to collect it, how to keep it manageable. Above all, try not to get bogged down in dry-as-dust facts; too much information is almost as bad as too little. A slow, step-by-step approach, while you learn to cope with large amounts of unfamiliar information, is a good way forward. You do not need the expertise of a qualified accountant to achieve success. Start modestly, with one daily newspaper with financial coverage, the weekly *Investors Chronicle*, one quality Sunday paper with a financial section, a quarterly subscription to either *Company REFS* or *The Estimate Directory*, one or two newsletters and the (free) annual reports from companies that take your interest.

Good information is worth more than money in the bank.

ESSENTIAL READING

There are a few items I would reckon to be absolutely essential research material. First, one daily newspaper which reports on finance and business, preferably in a separate section from the main newspaper. My choice is the *Financial Times*, as it has more extensive company coverage than any other daily paper. The daily *FT* is packed with vital facts for keeping tabs on the market. There are also major articles on topical aspects of markets, industries, companies and countries.

My husband complains the *FT* looks at everything mainly from a money rather than a news viewpoint. But for everyday financial facts I think it is unbeatable. If you prefer a daily with news items, buy the Saturday *FT* as a compromise, for it covers most of the main preceding week's events and often has interesting feature articles, usually with an overview on some highly topical subjects. An added bonus is the useful quarterly supplements on personal finance.

A Sunday newspaper is another good source of financial and company information, for example, *The Mail on Sunday* with its financial supplement, as these papers carry major features with plenty of background information on highly topical issues. They also give share tips, which can be followed up with FASTER GAINS.

The *Investors Chronicle* is a weekly journal with many interesting features, including analysis of market trends and foreign markets. It covers all company results in the week they are announced, which is a must for every investor. *Investors Chronicle* is currently the only financial journal that presents in one tidy package all the fundamental factors needed to follow the FASTER GAINS formula.

These appear in a handy format under each individual company results entry.

> *There is a treasure trove of small companies*
> *with giant growth prospects, waiting to be discovered*
> *by the diligent searcher.*

For me, the *Money Observer* magazine is a useful mini-reference source. It has special features and interesting articles and gives current interest rates for major banks and building societies. I have subscribed to it since I first began investing to benefit from the impressive coverage of all the investment areas I follow. Each month has a complete list of every quoted share, unit and investment trust. For a modest annual outlay, you get 23 pages of statistics on them all, with tables for a one-, six-month and one-year performance. This is a handy way to find shares or trusts that perform consistently well.

SIFTING FOR FASTER GAINS

When I began, these four items were my basic tools. If funds are tight, I would stick to those before indulging in extras. Now my equipment is more extensive and I have a good routine for sifting out the most promising companies to examine by FASTER GAINS. My first sieve is my favourite newsletters: *Chart Breakout* (using the breakout system of new highs, covered in Chapter 4); *Quantum Leap* (for small growth companies at an early stage of growth); *Techinvest* (for the technology and biotechnology sectors), and *Share Watch* (which covers extra-small companies). They alert me to interesting companies I have overlooked. If any company catches my eye, I put it on a custom page of my *Market Eye* screen, so I can follow the share price movements. Then I check analysts' forecasts in *The Estimate Directory* and the broad range of financial statistics in *Company REFS*. If I have doubts, I phone the company's registrars to order the latest reports; their telephone numbers appear in *The Estimate Directory* and *Company REFS*.

> *Newsletters can be a short cut to alert you to exciting*
> *shares you may not have noticed yet.*

Next, I print out both long- and short-term charts of the company's share price, to see how it has been performing over several years and in the last few months. Then I use FASTER GAINS. There are few cases where everything is perfect, so a judgement has now to be made. I may decide to buy or keep watching for a while, read the company report and see how the share price performs before making a decision.

TOP-UP RESEARCH TOOLS

Choice on reference sources for private investors has grown recently with the arrival of *Company REFS*. This is a comprehensive guide on almost all quoted UK companies including the new Alternative Investment Market (AIM). New subscribers receive a free companion book written by Jim Slater on how to use the astonishing bounty of statistics it contains. A simpler starter's approach is *The Estimate Directory*; data is more limited with broker and analyst forecasts on a smaller range of companies, leaving out many small firms, and some key fundamental analysis. Quarterly subscriptions are available on both these sources. For beginners *The Estimate Directory* is perhaps a gentler introduction, but *Company REFS* is far more extensive. The Extel financial companies service is a third source often to be found in main public libraries.

However, in my early days with just my starter's pack of one daily and Sunday financial newspaper, *Investors Chronicle* and *Money Observer*, I made encouraging profits. Doing the main research is the route to success. You can make handsome profits if you concentrate on the key facts and figures that get prominent attention in these four essential items and apply a broad stock-picking system like FASTER GAINS to any companies that sound worth investigating further. I'll let Peter Lynch have the final say on this essential secret for investment success. He was manager of the highly successful Fidelity Magellan Fund (a mutual fund, the American equivalent of British unit trusts) from 1977 until he retired in 1990.

Investing without research is like playing stud poker and never looking at the cards. Peter Lynch

TOP TIPS

There are plenty of newsletters to choose from, covering everything from small companies, **option trading**, technology shares, directors' share dealings, long-term growth shares or those with promising charts. They advertise widely in the financial press and offer special trial discounts to new subscribers. Using newsletters is a highly personal aid to investing. The four I have found most invaluable, as mentioned above, are *Quantum Leap* and *Chart Breakout*, both edited by Quentin Lumsden, *Techinvest* and *Sharewatch*.

Another good source of detailed information on markets and companies is *Analyst* magazine. It has wide and in-depth items on companies as well as general features. I began subscribing to *Analyst* in April 1990. In the September issue Jim Slater described his favourite stock-picking routines. This was a true turning point for me as a novice investor; it set me off on the search for small companies with giant prospects. A new magazine, *Stockmarket Solutions*, gives a full quarterly guide on shopping for investment aids and similar products.

ARMCHAIR AIDS

As a guide for novice investors, I rate the value of my research tools for the armchair investor like this: *Company REFS* and *Investors Chronicle* are my armchair accountants, with a tremendously broad coverage of essential financial information; *The Estimate Directory* is my armchair **broker**, giving forecasts on future profitability; newspapers are my armchair Reuters, updating me with all the vital news, and newsletters are my armchair **analysts**, alerting me to companies they have researched and about which they feel optimistic.

One reason for using expensive equipment is that it is an easy target to blame if things go wrong.

INFORMATION FROM THE HORSE'S MOUTH

Last, but by no means least, there is one source of information that is free and often neglected. The company itself is a rich source of information to inquisitive investors. You can telephone the company registrar to order the last published interim or annual report and, as a shareholder, you can go to the annual general meeting and listen to what the directors have to say. You can ask the company registrars broad questions about the company, or telephone directly and speak to the public relations department or the finance director. How a company handles your enquiries gives a good insight into their mode of operation and efficiency.

> *Why reinvent the wheel when there is so much available knowledge for you to use?*

Do not get frustrated if the financial accounts are unreadable. You learn the main signposts to look for as you progress. They say Rome wasn't built in a day, and building real wealth is a similar patient, one-step-after-another exercise. In *One Up On Wall Street*, Peter Lynch has a guide in plain English on how to read a company's accounts. Newsletters are another route to identifying the crucial facts for a profitable investment. The editor gives several reasons, based on the company's accounts, for buying or selling a share. Newsletters with a good track record for picking winners are a useful short cut for beginners. They usually list their current paper portfolios, so you can see how successful they are. *Caution is the big buzz word here. Yesterday's successes may not be repeated tomorrow.* It is hard to remember, but we are always looking for tomorrow's big winners, not today's. When you tackle the company's annual reports, even if the actual figures mean nothing to you, the chairman's and chief executive's reports will give you insights into the company's plans and progress.

OUT AND ABOUT

Sometimes you can make company visits. Everyone can visit the publicly quoted supermarkets, retailers and football clubs, to see how they are operating. I was interested in Denby, the pottery manufacturer which floated on the stock market in the summer of 1994. A few weeks before the float, I went on a visitors' tour of the factory, which gave me some valuable clues about its prospects.

Another useful way to obtain information is to attend the frequently held money shows and conferences catering specially for small private investors. They offer plenty of material to mull over plus the opportunity to ask questions of knowledgeable people. Attending these conferences is profitable for face-to-face fact-finding. Although I listen to ideas about good shares, I try to avoid acting on 'tips' from people 'in the know' and this includes my newsletters. If I hear something useful, I always go through the stages listed above, and monitor the share for a while, before making a decision.

Research you have paid for should never be dumped, until you are fully convinced you have finished with it.

USING THE INFORMATION

Buying research material is never cheap, so the worst possible thing to do is to dump it in the waste basket after you have read it. From the outset, try to use this paper mountain as your facts databank, to build up reference files of key financial facts on the companies and markets you follow. This applies to newspapers as well as to the journals. I keep the whole week's *FT* 'Companies and Markets' section until the next weekend, in case I missed a company with very good results which I might later think worth investing in. This is vital with recovery shares, where the latest set of results may help me decide when all the bad news is finally behind it, but I may have missed that good news during the week. I also tear off and file the back two pages of the *FT* 'Companies and Markets' section every day, except Monday. These two pages record all the key statistics on the UK quoted companies. Storing these builds up a useful ready reference for checking back on specific details at any time in the future.

As soon as the dustman has emptied your bin, you will want a news item you missed or forgot to cut out.

CUTTINGS FOR KEEPS

I keep newspaper cuttings on the companies I follow, either because I am a shareholder or may buy their shares in the near future. My filing system is simple, just a few plastic folders; one for items on shares I hold and another on shares which are possible 'buys'. I keep a file of interesting articles covering the sectors I watch; currently this includes the media and technology sectors. I store all the *Investors Chronicles*, right back to 1990, so I can refer to a back issue. Of course, I keep all my newsletters. As the paper collection grows, hoarding newsletters is a good test for deciding which of them are indispensable and which are no longer earning their shelf space.

Occasionally I have a sort out, to discard cuttings on companies I no longer follow and store old journals in the garage. I sort through my paper mountain in the week before a holiday. This is the only time my office is tidy. On my return the papers start piling up again, because I arrange for the newsagent to save all the *FTs* and *The Mail on Sundays* while I am away. Then I take a week or so to read quickly through them and keep up with all the major news as well as any important company results that occurred in my absence. My cuttings files get updated, with no gaps. And, of course, the newsletters go on arriving, even while I am away.

Always find shelf space for your research items, until you are convinced you will never refer to them again.

THE LONELINESS OF THE LONG-TERM INVESTOR

While it is obvious that the *Financial Times, Investors Chronicle* plus a quality Sunday paper would all count as essential research material, what information, apart from the tips, is gained from the newsletters? Armchair investors have many advantages over nine-to-five office slaves, but working in the peace and tranquillity of your own home can be lonely if you have no one with whom to discuss your ideas. This is where the newsletters score. To me, they are knowledgeable investment friends who unfailingly come calling once a month. They bring me their latest views on the current scene. But instead of a friendly chat, everything they want to tell me is written down, so I can refer to it several times over. I know how much I value them when I find myself working out how many days I must wait until their next publication day. I am never lonely on days when a favourite up-to-date newsletter arrives.

Why are they indispensable? First, they often draw my attention to facts about the current market situation that I may not have known. They give measured views on recent results of companies they follow. They make special company visits that would be a hopeless task for me personally, as they know better which important questions to ask at these visits. Then, again, they alert me to companies that will have results in the next few weeks, so I can make a quick buy or sell decision when those results are released. And finally, they give me very broad background information on companies they personally favour.

Let your newsletters do the heavy research. Then you take it forward, to the final buy or sell decision.

Not every choice is attractive, but from this monthly list, I choose shares I want to follow. In short, a good newsletter is the nearest small private investors get to copying professional fund managers. The newsletter editor is your own personal broker/analyst, offering expert advice for a fee.

CLUB TOGETHER

One excellent alternative to working alone is to join or form a local investment club in your area. This is highly popular among American private investors, but far less widespread here. It certainly allows plenty of scope for a healthy exchange of ideas and some clubs have made tremendous profits. The famous Beardstown Ladies Club made such consistently good returns over twelve years, they actually wrote a book about their methods and their success; in 1991 alone, their portfolio leapt by 60 per cent. Tony Drury's book *Investment Clubs – the low-risk way to stockmarket profits* gives plenty of advice on how to get started and which useful investment tools to acquire. Obviously, expensive reference subscriptions will be cheaper per person when shared between several serious investors.

It is perfectly possible to make super profits with the absolute minimum of special investment aids.

OPTIONAL EXTRAS

When I first started I didn't have a software package for preparing ready-made charts or keeping a record of my deals. I made my charts by the unbelievably time-consuming process of manually collecting figures from the *FT* and then drawing out the chart on graph paper. This drudgery meant tracking through a two-year record of closing prices at my local library. Each day, I calculated the three moving averages I kept for the FT-SE 100 chart. These will be explained in Chapter 4.

This is not a choice I would cheerfully recommend to novices, as quarterly charts are available from several sources to avoid this truly burdensome task. My complete lack of sophisticated aids simply stresses the point that they are not indispensable for making profits. My experience shows that on the scale of the initial necessary costs incurred, discussed earlier in the chapter, I was willing to devote much more time and effort than hard cash to my research. Nor did I own a real-time machine, like a *Market Eye* system, for instant share prices. I began with no updated price data at all. Then I started frugally, using the *FT Cityline* telephone price service.

My trappist monk's approach, costing few pennies, was, I now realize, hugely expensive in time and effort. There are far better ways of doing things if I had known how. Nonetheless, with this frugal plan, by March 1992 my total portfolio had grown after two full years by a moderately healthy 21 per cent. This was achieved after the portfolio had climbed painfully back to my starting point, so it had to recover the 7 per cent I lost in my first six months, before the profits began.

WEALTH WARNING: if your portfolio falls by 50 per cent, then it will have to grow by 100 per cent just to put you back to where you began.

Teletext is a useful help to obtain share prices, but they are not real-time prices. *Market Eye* and *Reuters* both provide real-time prices. Unless you have plenty of cash, the step-by-step approach is a better route. Use any spare cash to increase your investment kitty, and once you begin making profits you can start collecting some additional items. The problem of where to start in this minefield of optional extras has now been addressed with *Stockmarket Solutions*.

A BEVY OF BROKERS

Finally, you have to select a stockbroker before you can get started, although this can wait if you begin with a paper portfolio as explained in Chapter 5. *Investors Chronicle* and the financial sections of newspapers regularly cover the full range of stockbrokers. This information is obtainable from the London Stock Exchange. Briefly, there are two main types of broker offering services; execution only and advisory brokers. Execution only brokers do not give advice but will give you factual information on companies. To keep costs down for clients, the services on offer may be spartan. But you can buy shares with as little as £200, by post for a £5 commission fee. This is the cheapest available route to share ownership, but postal delays and processing your order in the broker's office mean you have no control over the price at which you buy. I would not recommend this route but you can use telephone ordering through execution only brokers for buying a small investment. With some brokerage firms, the cost starts at £10 but rises with the amount you spend.

Become your own broker; take your own advice.

All the major banks offer share dealing services, and a visit to your local branch will give you your first brochure on what brokers offer. If you feel happier receiving professional advice before plunging in, this is a perfectly sensible route to take. I was quite happy to start with my bank broker. I received their monthly newsletter and took their advice, for a modest fee, until I felt I could manage better alone. I used their services for more than a year and do not begrudge the costs incurred. Every step on the route to success has to be paid for, in time, effort or in hard cash.

Every aspect of investing needs monitoring for beginners and old hands alike. This applies to brokers. I changed brokers three times before I found one I was happy to use for everything. Yes, that does mean I used four different brokers. Some people suggest using two brokers in tandem, for flexibility. I did this during my first year, as I was unhappy with the brokers. However, after about fifteen months, I began using my present broker. I prefer to have just one really efficient broker who gets to know all my requirements and is able to offer me the best all-round service. But that is my personal preference. The way I decided it was time to move on was when I experienced hassles which were troublesome to resolve with a supervisor or manager. Be absolutely determined not to accept poor service, as there is now a healthy competition for your business and you should expect a good service, however infrequently you use the broker.

OWNERSHIP MATTERS

Major changes are under way in the share settlement process; the leisurely two-week account system was jettisoned to ensure all deals, both purchases and sales, are settled in a much shorter time. The first phase of ten-day settlement shrank to five-day rolling settlement. In practice, this means if you pay for shares by cheques in the post, the almost certain delays will involve you in extra costs. Your cheque is unlikely to reach the broker in time for him to effect settlement on your behalf. If he has to finance the settlement before your cheque clears, you will bear the added cost. The solution is to leave money on deposit with the broker, if he is organized for that. The alternative is the all-embracing answer, a nominee account. Here, the shares are held by the broker on the shareholder's behalf. Like the curate's egg, this system is good, but only in parts.

The broker handles all the tiresome paperwork for you and holds your shares in a nominee account which proves your ownership of them. Provided you use a broker with a *huge insurance policy* (not just *adequate* cover, which may prove to be quite inadequate if disaster does strike), this is a satisfactory way to handle the new settlement system. In fact, everyone who has a Personal Equity Plan (PEP) is technically using a 'nominee account', because the Inland Revenue insist every plan is held and controlled only by authorized brokers.

You will be more likely to make wise decisions, if you are always alert to the rare chance that the nightmare scenario can suddenly become reality.

I use nominee accounts myself and do not feel unduly disadvantaged by the shortcomings often quoted in the press. These include the problem that they are not authorized under the Financial Services Act and so are technically not covered by the Investors' Compensation Scheme. Hence the vital need to ensure the broker you entrust with your valuable share certificates has a massive insurance policy, so you have adequate cover.

The other disadvantage with nominee accounts is the technical loss of ownership, although at present my broker makes beneficial ownership possible. This means ownership is still acknowledged to be mine, so I receive information from companies in which I have shares, including annual and interim reports, information on rights issues and other news items, and the right to attend company meetings. My broker makes no charges for this privilege, or for collecting dividends or sending me company information, but I have lost the company perks, with discounts on this, that or the other. I am not investing for discounts; I want to put my money into companies with the prospects of seeing it double in five years, or so. To me, discounts don't matter. However, in July 1996 the new Crest settlement system came into effect. Crest is designed to computerize the settlement of buying and selling shares and to eventually eliminate share certificates entirely. At the time of writing, this system is as yet unproven and it is impossible to say how it will ultimately affect small private shareholders as views on how it will operate in practice vary considerably among the different parties involved. We shall just have to decide how we want to deal with our portfolios once we have some actual experience of it.

Now we have assembled a minimum tool-kit and have all this valuable research information at our fingertips. We have seen how to use it with FASTER GAINS to choose super stocks. I'll tell you how I use charts for timing buy and sell signals in the next chapter.

Money can buy you anything, except common sense.

CHAPTER 4

Profitable clues from charts

When jittery investors are bailing out at the bottom, you should be happy to relieve them of their burdensome shares.

Fundamentalists may doubt the value of charts but I use both fundamental and technical analysis to gather as much information as possible. Opportunities arise for making splendid gains, *if we can spot that the conditions are right.*

Technical analysts watch price movements on charts as they believe the charts reveal the collective behaviour of all investors. So they search for repeating price patterns. Spotting these at an early stage offers the prospect of gains, selling to protect paper profits, or to control losses, if a similar move unfolds. Technical analysis also covers a range of market statistics, which operate like a temperature gauge for market activity. We can use this cluster of facts to interpret the past actions and motives of investors. When favourable patterns re-emerge, if we understand what they mean, we can profit from them.

However, no single technical fact is infallible. The best occasions usually arise when several indicators give the same signal together; one alone is unreliable. When many signals point the same way, you have a better chance of being right. If a promising chart pattern appears, we look for other confirmatory signals. Each situation can produce a variety of outcomes, so even if one yielded a profitable result, repeat performances are not guaranteed. Using confirmatory signals reduces the likelihood of inadvertently acting in situations that may throw up these unwelcome diverging outcomes.

Some chart patterns give clues for major turning points in a share price or an index because they indicate a change of sentiment by a large group of investors. These are studied by technical analysts to determine when to buy or sell. However, like a Picasso painting, we cannot expect to understand the mystifying messages in his art unless we know the jargon. Similarly, if we learn technical analysis jargon, we can exploit profitable opportunities as they arise in the markets.

> *and where is the use of a book, thought Alice,*
> *without pictures . . . ?* Lewis Carroll

I always use fundamental analysis for investment decisions, but I study charts of both stock market indices and individual share prices to spot repeating patterns. I think they reflect the recurring crowd behaviour of investor populations just as a pressure chart shows weather patterns or a temperature chart monitors a patient's progress.

AVOID THE DRIFT

Traders complain that markets go through frustrating 'do-nothing' phases. They spend long periods drifting aimlessly and only infrequently move positively, either up or down. This annoying behaviour explains why investing without adequate preparation is most unwise. Weeks of discouraging drifting may be followed by a swift, unexpected rally, which is almost over before your action plan is in place. A drifting market is a poor environment for making profits, so judging when it might switch from sluggish to active is helpful for separating out unprofitable from profitable opportunities.

When structure appears in the market, we can make profits.

SECRET STRUCTURES

During the drift periods, chart patterns are often shapeless, but the market is forever changing and, periodically, structure appears. The emergence of structure is often a reliable sign that drifting is coming to an end; it implies market movements are getting orderly and hence might be more predictable. If we see 'structure' patterns and know what the structure is signalling we can exploit our new-found insight. Structure in the markets is the financial equivalent of a magician's conjuring trick. Like magic, it seems to appear out of nothing, but the skill is to understand the 'know-how' involved. Structure is virtually everywhere in the markets: in base-formations, trading ranges, breakouts, rectangles, support and resistance levels, trends, channels, flags and gaps. In this chapter I will cover only those few key signs of structure that I rely on, but many simple books are available, explaining how to use charts in more detail. David Linton's *Profit From Your PC* is a good primer.

BASE-BUILDING

The market consists of optimists and pessimists; their conflicting views on the future are like two tug-of-war teams. Each is always pulling in the opposite direction from the other. This divergence creates the market for trading shares but on numerous occasions the two teams are indecisive and the pulling action becomes blurred.

There are only two kinds of investor; the natural optimists and the natural pessimists.

The first visible sign of structure to note on a chart is a base-building phase. It forms when buyers (optimists) and sellers (pessimists) are evenly matched. The price may be static for weeks, months or even years, because neither group can force the share price to move in a decisive direction. Sometimes, and for the same reason, buyers matching sellers creates a trading range, with narrow, see-saw moves between two prices (shown for Hanson, the international conglomerate group, in Figure 4). Trading ranges, discussed below, are further evidence of structure.

Most base-building or trading ranges finally end with a breakout, either upwards or downwards. A breakout is a strong signal to buy (if the price breaks up), or sell (if it breaks down). Breakouts show the bulls (optimists) or bears (pessimists) have at last forced the price to move in one direction. They are the third positive sign of structure in the market. You can be confident that base-forming or the trading range is over only if the chart makes a very pronounced upwards or downwards move away from it. A decisive breakout influenced my Unipalm purchase; the Unipalm chart (Figure 17, p. 95) shows the breakout after a long base-building phase. The buy signal at B, at a price above 144–5p, occurred as the long base-building phase ended.

BEAUTIFUL BREAKOUTS

When there are more buyers than sellers, a share price or index breaks up from its trading range. A breakout on high volume (many buyers) is a strong signal to buy. Cautious investors wait until a price is 2 or 3 per cent *above the old high*, to confirm it as a true breakout. Conversely, if an index breaks down from a long trading phase, it is a signal to sell. For adventurous investors, taking out a 'put' option contract after a breakdown can be profitable as the lower level of the trading range now becomes a firm resistance barrier to any up-thrust of the movement once the price has decisively broken down away from it.

This pattern is clearly seen on the Hanson price chart, in Figure 4. The price was locked in a trading range, forming a long rectangle, between prices at around 190p to 250p from 1989 to 1993. It then broke out firmly on the up-side, before collapsing back again below the resistance line which held at 250p in August 1995, to touch 186p during November 1995.

The famous speculator Jesse Livermore made a fortune using the breakout system on Wall Street during the early decades of the century. He made his best gains when he exercised strict discipline, waiting until the true breakout was confirmed. He knew acting ahead of the signal is risky and produces unpredictable results. His account describes typical market drift as 'the get-nowhere prices', and he identified the trading range by 'the limits of the get-nowhere prices'. He gave this advice for using breakout buy and sell signals: 'There is no sense trying to anticipate the next big movement, whether it is going to be up or down. The thing to do is to watch the market to determine the limits of the get-nowhere prices and make up your mind that you will not take an interest until prices break through the limits in either direction.'

Markets constantly throw up useful clues for those with the right antennae to receive them.

AVOID SIGNS OF MARKET AMBIGUITY

Directionless phases create endless market drift. Chart formations of base areas, rectangles, or a defined trading range show delays before either buyers or sellers control the action. These phases are termed congestion areas. Rectangles are marked on charts for the FT-SE 100 (Figure 5) and the Nasdaq Composite indices (Figure 6). Drifting markets are the most uncertain and hence risky for making profits, but are excellent periods for planning what to buy for your portfolio.

The rectangle pattern represents areas of trading where two stable prices exist, one at each end of the range. It is a box within which the buyers and sellers have staged a fairly even contest, with neither group an outright winner. The rectangle, like base-building and a trading range, is another sign of structure, but it is ambiguous; we cannot predict the actual outcome, until the price finally breaks out of the rectangle. When a rectangle trading range

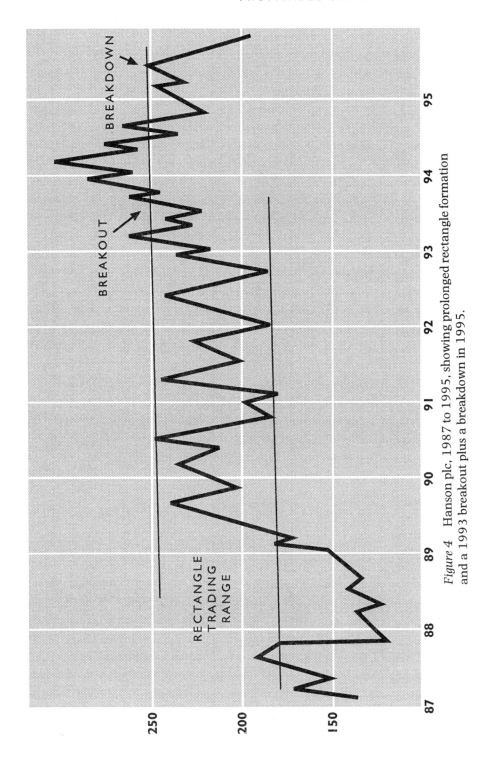

Figure 4 Hanson plc, 1987 to 1995, showing prolonged rectangle formation and a 1993 breakout plus a breakdown in 1995.

65

develops, the lower line becomes a support level, where buyers enter the market, and the upper level offers resistance as they sell out. The box made by a rectangle pattern has a lower support level, where buyers appear, and an upper resistance level when profit-taking occurs.

> *Markets are driven by news or too much money*
> *chasing too few stocks.*

Support and resistance lines are further evidence of structure, indicating the current strength of buying or selling pressures. When the line is finally broken, by a decisive move either up or down, it indicates the resolution of the tussle between buyers and sellers. This is another good clue to the likely turn of events, as the move will usually be strong enough to continue for some time in the same direction. As we saw, I used this support concept with my investment in Medeva at a price around 200p in March 1995.

SIGNALS FROM MOVING AVERAGES

A helpful way to identify structure is to put moving averages on your charts. Moving averages are lagging indicators; they follow rather than lead the price. They do not predict movements, but they help to confirm them. The calculation is done by averaging a price over a set number of days. On each successive day, the latest figure is added and the oldest figure in the previous day's calculation drops out.

> *Buy and sell clues appear as a price bounces*
> *off a moving average.*

I use moving averages in twos or threes, to give buy or sell clues, as one moving average alone is a poor indicator; they work best in groups of three; short, medium and longer-term duration. A short moving average might cover 5, 10 or 20 days; a medium average would cover 30, 40 or 50 days, while a long-term average covers 90, 100 or 200 days. Different technicians prefer different time scales. Moving averages smooth out random daily fluctuations in

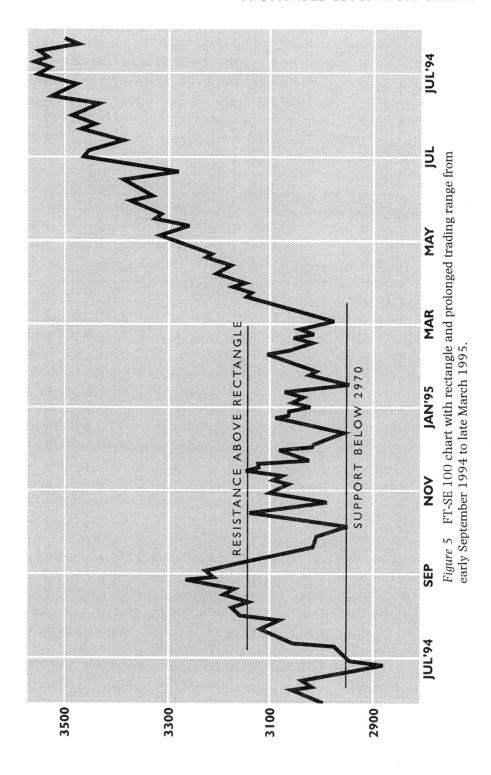

Figure 5 FT-SE 100 chart with rectangle and prolonged trading range from early September 1994 to late March 1995.

CALCULATION OF A FIVE-DAY MOVING AVERAGE				
Date	FT-SE 100	Cum. total	No of days	5-day MA
1/9/95	3509.4		1	
4/9/95	3522.7		2	
5/9/95	3532.4		3	
6/9/95	3557.7		4	
7/9/95	3545.6	17667.8	5	3533.6
8/9/95	3554.5	17712.9	6	3542.6
11/9/95	3549.3	17730.5	7	3547.9
12/9/95	3535.9	17743.0	8	3548.6
13/9/95	3570.8	17756.1	9	3551.2
14/9/95	3565.4	17775.9	10	3555.2

the price; the reason they are helpful is because they isolate the underlying trend. This is another important sign denoting structure in the price movements.

STRONG BUY SIGNALS

Moving averages used in clusters of two or three, of varying durations, will give a good buy signal when a rising short-term average (say the 20-day) cuts up through a rising medium-term average (the 50-day). This creates a positive signal called a 'golden cross'. (The opposite, a 'dead cross' occurs when a falling short-term moving average cuts down through a falling longer-term average. This is a negative or sell signal.) As a 'golden cross' appears, if both averages now continue moving up one behind the other, the price is building a trend, giving a second bullish signal. If the longer-term, 200-day average also starts to turn up, after having been falling or flat for some time, this adds a third bullish signal to the other two. The three signals together confirm the bullish move, making it more reliable.

When all these three bullish signals are present together, a major turning point may be developing. The search for signs of major turning points in the market is vital to small investors. It is risky to make investments before a decisive turning point has actually occurred. This is what happens repeatedly to gullible small investors who get sucked into the market at a peak, or conversely,

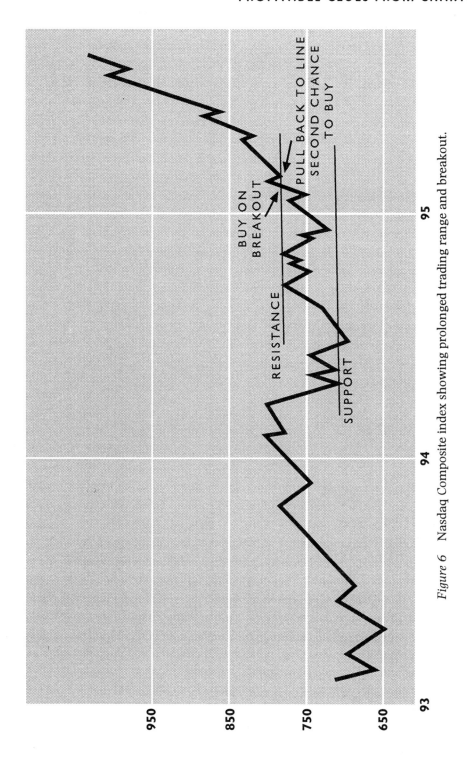

Figure 6 Nasdaq Composite index showing prolonged trading range and breakout.

finally dump their shares in a panic, right at the bottom of the market. If they took the trouble to learn and understand the signals in the charts, they could easily avoid this perverse and expensive investment behaviour.

For successful investing, follow the trend.

TREND SPOTTING

The best buy signals occur as a trend gets established. The trend appears on the chart when all three averages of different time scales are moving up in line, one behind the other, under the rising share price. As the trend develops, an investment now could produce good results. After a breakout from a trading or a base-building period, the developing trend is clearly seen on many charts. From time to time, the price line of an index or share drops back again to make contact with one of its averages (the 20-day, 50-day or 200-day average). After a contact, the price might bounce up off the average and continue up, but it might fall below the average if the trend is losing momentum.

Examples of buy signals from some of these features appear in Figure 7, for the Dow Jones Industrial Average from May 1994 to August 1995. There was base-building and a break up, two golden crosses, three moving averages rising in line, one behind the other, the 200-day average turned up in January 1995, and the index line hugged the 20-day moving average (moving up from it and falling back to it), in March, April, May, June and July 1995. In August, the index fell to make contact with the 50-day moving average, before rising up off it again.

The index was locked in a trading range between 3,675 and 3,950 until the end of January 1995. However, all three moving averages, 20-, 50- and 200-day, were bunched together in December 1994. This bunching is often a sign of an imminent breakout, because structure appears when the trend and three averages cluster together; *all the surface randomness has momentarily disappeared.* On the Dow, the 20-day average rose through the other two, forming two golden crosses over the Christmas holiday. In January 1995, the 200-day moving average began to turn

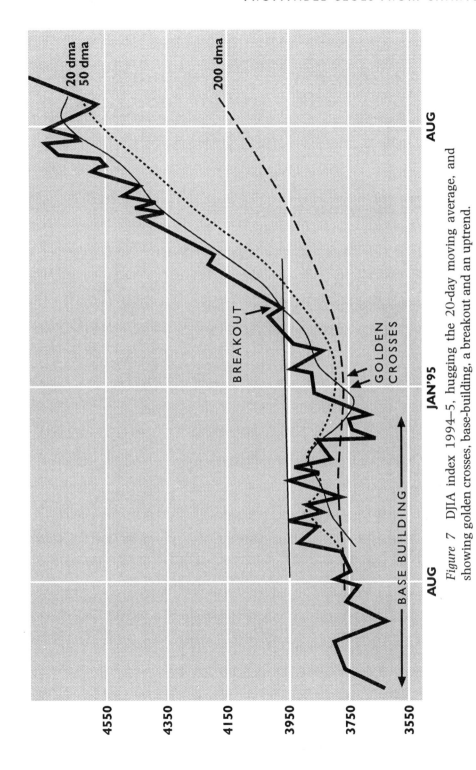

Figure 7 DJIA index 1994–5, hugging the 20-day moving average, and showing golden crosses, base-building, a breakout and an uptrend.

upwards and the index then went on to breakout above the base-range in mid-February to reach 4,000 by the end of February. As the trend was established, two good confirmatory signals emerged: first, the three moving averages were moving up in line, one behind the other; second, by May, we could draw a channel for the index, with the top line joining the upper highs and the bottom line joining the lows.

PROFIT FROM THE TREND

Trends are further evidence of structure in the market. Share price rises encourage more buying and further price rises, and the trend grows through this self-perpetuating loop. When the market is rising, everyone wants to buy. Short bouts of profit-taking may occur, but in a strong trend the up-move quickly reaserts itself as new buyers enter the market. Prices are pushed ever higher, but the trend grows increasingly unstable until a bout of intense profit-taking emerges and the mood swings abruptly in the opposite direction. Heavy selling brings out more sellers and prices fall, stimulating further selling.

When everyone is buying, the market leaps for joy.

Big profits can accumulate by staying with a prolonged rising trend. After the Dow Jones broke out of its trading range in December 1994, the trend lasted for six months. At the end of August 1995, the 20-day and 50-day moving averages made a dead cross and the index fell below its trend line but held at the 50-day moving average. It recovered during September, making another golden cross as it rose towards a new, all-time high of 4,800. This dead cross seemed a sell signal, but it was not confirmed. The index fell but did not stay below its 50-day average. In fact, the index bounced up briskly from that level.

However, even the most long-lived trend eventually comes to an end. It cuts down below the 50-day average and may find support at the lower 200-day average or fall even lower. After a sustained run, it is crucial to protect the profits you have made, unless you feel confident the story supporting your favourite company share price has much further to run. If you are holding shares you want to sell to reinvest in a more promising company, it is helpful if you can judge whether the trend is now going to turn decisively down for a while.

TIMING THE TURN

It is best to wait for firm evidence before acting after a long run up in the index, as it may drop a little and then continue even higher. This happened with the Dow Jones index during the autumn of 1995, and it reached the 5,000 level by mid-November. It is a frequent occurrence for a price to hover around one level for quite a while, so that both the short- and possibly the medium-term averages can catch up with the main price action. The pause indicates there is no clear winner between buyers or sellers. For a share or index in a strongly rising trend, the end of a sharp drop or catch-up pause gives another buy signal as the price begins to bounce up after touching an average.

Wait patiently for the confirmatory signals to appear and avoid the high risk ambiguous phases.

When this pattern appears on a chart it suggests the bullish mood will continue, with new buyers willing to enter the market after a bout of profit-taking. These clues show why watching the price in relation to its moving averages gives better buy signals. The optimum buy signal occurs when the price actually starts to bounce up from the average, as seen in Figure 7, where the American Dow Jones Industrial Average index was repeatedly bouncing up off its 20-day moving average during 1994–5, and fell back to meet its 50-day average in August 1995, before bouncing up again as the rising trend continued.

STRONG SELL SIGNALS

Conversely, be extra vigilant when a share or an index has risen extremely fast and stands a very long way above all three moving averages. If this happens during a strong boom, it may signal the arrival of a peak. An adverse event now, which seems to upset many investors, can prompt more profit-taking. If you think this is imminent, you should sell up to 25 per cent of your portfolio on the assumption that this unfavourable event might trigger a major turning point. If the market does now fall, a large decline may follow, retracing perhaps 15 to 25 per cent of the huge previous rise.

To protect profits from that eventuality, watch closely for any sign that other technical indicators are giving confirmatory negative signals. If they do, further profit-taking in the portfolio is a sound precaution. Some technical indicators that offer clues to a setback at the peak are described in Chapter 6. The way moving averages behave can help in giving these additional signals. A second 25 per cent of the portfolio should be sold if the falling shorter, 20-day moving average cuts down below a falling longer-term average (50-day). This is a 'dead cross' pattern and is the opposite formation to the bullish signal, a 'golden cross'. Clearly, a dead cross is a negative signal; it confirms the continuing fall and indicates a sell decision.

THE MARKET IS FOR TURNING

Moving average analysis is not the only direct guidance available for timing profitable opportunities. As we noted earlier, searching for major turning points is important, as they signify a big reversal in the mood of investors and therefore in chart patterns. A big turning point is accompanied by a **reversal pattern**. Spotting reversal signals enables you to sell early in an unfavourable market or buy early as a new up-trend emerges. The markets anticipate or discount most news items, so a struggle exists between reality and expectations. If good news is expected and it duly arrives, there may be no reaction. The market might even fall, as the good news has already been discounted. This is the reason why a company announcing wonderful results may see its share price drop. All the buying in expectation of this splendid result occurred in the weeks of run-up before the results.

No one single investment aid is infallible.

BENEFICIAL TRENDS

But if bad news is expected and the news is good, market reaction can be swift and excessive, with optimism surging. Prices begin moving predominantly in one direction as the big professionals enter the market in strength. The final outcome can create an extreme overshoot. But if the fundamental factors have been improved by this unexpected news, and the forecasts look good, a new bull trend arrives. This is one of the most profitable formations that asset markets produce. Powerful up-trends repeatedly emerge in bond, commodity and currency markets, as well as in stock markets.

Once established, a trend can last for weeks, months, years or decades. The duration depends upon the time frame being used. It can link with the four-year political cycle, the eight-year business cycle, or the forty- to fifty-year prolonged cycle of rising prosperity seen in the West since 1945. When it has settled in, whether a trend lasts one, four or eight years, it offers the chance to make superb profits with lower risk, at least until the trend is broken. The existence of a strong up-trend is one of the most solid market structures to develop. It emerges through the circularity of a buying loop, as buying encourages more buying. The strong up-trend is ratchet-shaped; usually two spurts up followed by one down. Its jagged pattern has a series of rising highs, which turn down when profit-taking begins, and rising lows, marking the point where buying increases again after a bout of profit-taking.

A good up-trend in a share is confirmed if its accompanying relative strength chart also shows an up-trend. The relative strength line charts the movement of the price relative to the whole market. A weakening in the relative strength is a warning sign of a possible change in the trend. A line joining the tops and bottoms of the chart creates the up- or downward channel in which the trend travels. The number of points making contact with the two lines measures the strength of the trend. Only a few contact points indicate a weaker signal than on a trend with plenty of contacts. Charts of price lines moving within a well-defined channel are shown in Figure 8 for the FT-SE 100 index, Figure 9 for Coda, a small software company, and Figure 10 for Filtronic Comtek, a small mobile telecom manufacturer.

LONG-TERM TRENDS

There were long, six-year bull trends in the 1920s and 1980s, both ending in crashes, in 1929 and 1987. Japan's surging bull market survived through almost two decades. The astonishing world economic growth, post-World War II, with greater democracy, increasing international trade and rising wealth, has produced a phenomenal long-term rise in all the stock markets of the main western industrial nations. George Blakey, in *The Post-War History of The London Stock Market, 1945 to 1992*, records the long-run growth of many giant multinational UK companies, including Hanson, Racal, BTR and Tomkins. In Britain, the FT Industrial Ordinary 30 Share index rose from 105.9 at the start of August 1945 to 2,791 by 31 May 1996. The Dow Jones Industrial Average shows an even greater rise, from 125 on 1 August 1945 to 5,643 by 31 May 1996. Looking back to 1896, when the Dow was first compiled, it has risen more than 100-fold from 50 to 5,643.

Sometimes a fall in prices is a good buying opportunity.

SECULAR BULL TRENDS

Some American investors have become billionaires, profiting over decades from the remarkable growth in the American economy which brought huge leaps on the stock market over this prolonged period. The fabled Warren Buffett, America's second wealthiest man (after Bill Gates of Microsoft), has been in the forefront of this advance. His holding company is worth $29 billion, of which he and his wife own 44 per cent. Anyone smart enough to buy 40 shares at $20 dollars each in his fund in 1965 for an outlay of $800 would now be a millionaire. The performance of Fidelity's Magellan Fund under the stewardship of the legendary Peter Lynch

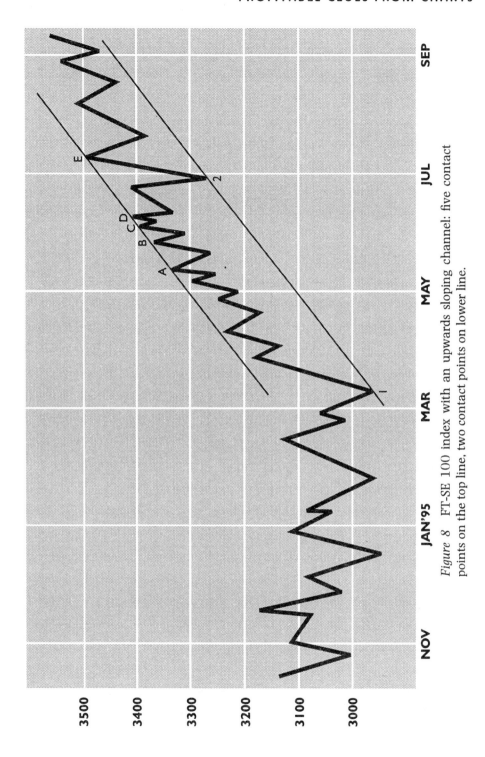

Figure 8 FT-SE 100 index with an upwards sloping channel: five contact points on the top line, two contact points on the lower line.

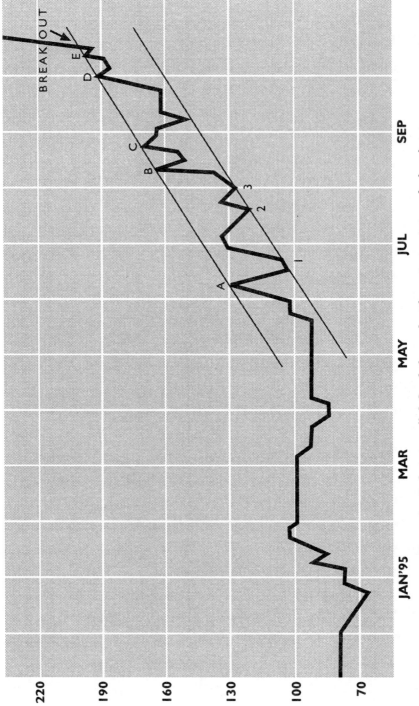

Figure 9 Coda in a well-defined channel with contact points and a breakout.

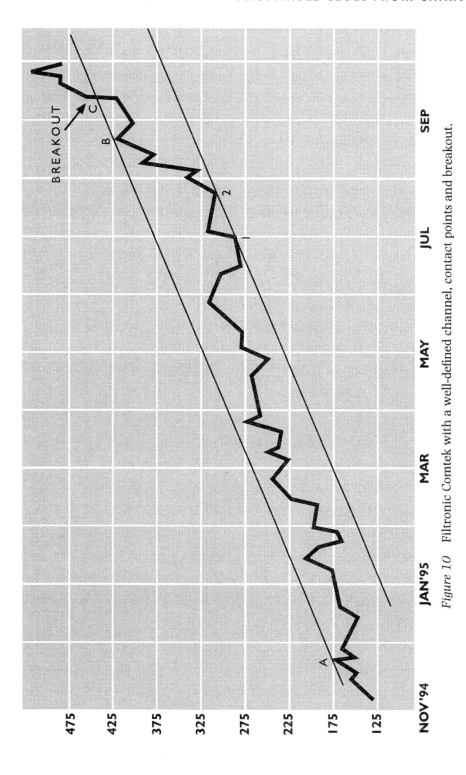

Figure 10 Filtronic Comtek with a well-defined channel, contact points and breakout.

was equally amazing. The chart in Figure 11, of Magellan over the last 13 years, shows the growth consistency under the impulse of a long term up-trend, operating through this period.

The performances of star investors like Warren Buffett and Peter Lynch confirm what could be achieved over the past few decades. What we need to know is if these optimistic long-term trends will continue. An article in August 1995, by Canada's RBC Dominion Securities in their *Strategic Review*, 'US Market' section, offers an interesting viewpoint on this question. It comments on the idea of secular bull trends. These are periodic trends, occurring over the long term. They operate over extensive periods in market sectors experiencing exceptional growth. Historically, secular leadership is evident in all major bull cycles, within a strongly rising trend.

The article suggests secular leadership extends beyond one normal business cycle of four years because it reflects the fundamental growth potentials of the leading edge sector. In the 1970s this was energy, and the up-trend lasted from 1961 to 1985; in the 1980s it was consumer goods and the trend lasted from 1970 to 1995. We currently may be at the start of a new prolonged secular trend tied to technology: computers, software, semiconductors, telecommunications equipment, biotechnology and pharmaceutical products.

A timely investment in a 'leading edge sector' share can reap rich rewards.

The secular trend has volatile bouts, which mirrors the mood swings of investors, from over-optimistic to over-pessimistic. Periodic declines of 15 to 25 per cent can occur but the recoveries are strong, taking the indices to new highs. Although there is early scepticism, it finally gives way to a stronger up-thrust since each recovery to new highs increases investor confidence. If this article is right, the mid-1995 bubble-like properties of the technology sectors may be deceptive, as there will be periodic strong recoveries after each short-term correction phase. And if the article is wrong, there is still no doubt in my mind that a well-prepared system for profiting from stock market investments is the best route to real wealth.

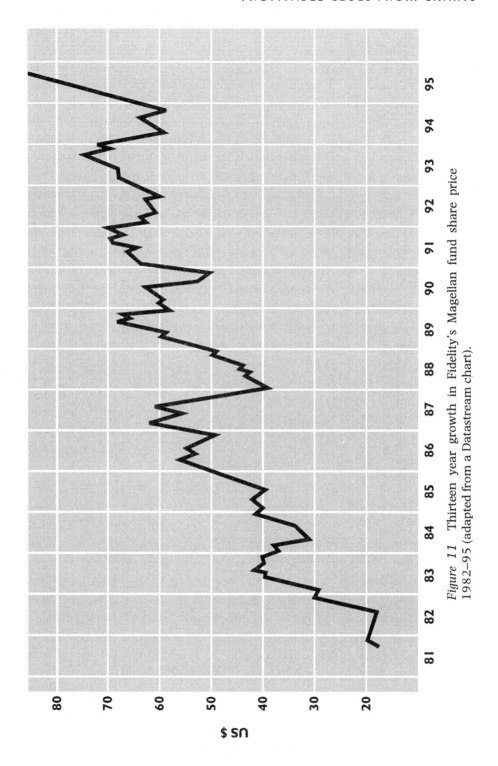

Figure 11 Thirteen year growth in Fidelity's Magellan fund share price 1982–95 (adapted from a Datastream chart).

BEFRIEND THE TREND

Trends of every length are further evidence of market structure. Alert investors can participate in these formative trends as they emerge. The Glaxo chart in Figure 12 shows short downward sliding channels at A and B, from which two healthy breakouts occurred, at C and D. At point E, a powerful up-channel developed and the up-trend continued after a rectangle-forming pause at F, to reach 1,850p (equivalent to 925p after the two-for-one split early in 1992) by February 1992. The later part of this rise is shown in Figure 13. The Glaxo surge was due to worldwide sales of its drug Zantac, for indigestion sufferers. It was the most profitable drug of the 1980s.

George Soros, one of the greatest speculators of the century, explains why super-profits come by following the trend. 'Short-term volatility [i.e. instability] is greatest at turning points and diminishes as a trend is established.' For this reason, the old market adage claims, 'The trend is your friend.'

The early stages of a new up-trend are the most profitable because the earlier you invest, the more investors there will be who follow your lead. Their arrival in strength helps to bid share prices way above the levels you paid for them. Young trends offer the best prospects for profit with lower levels of risk, because once established, a trend often feeds on itself, which gives it a useful longevity. The now-famous Beardstown Ladies Investment Club took advantage of this early trend-forming phase. In 1991, the first year after a recession pause on Wall Street, their portfolio grew by 59.5 per cent. Among their top investments was the UK giant drugs firm, Glaxo, still moving through its explosive growth stage.

The best gains usually occur in the first two years of a young bull market.

UK EUPHORIA

In the UK stock market an unexpected up-trend formation occurred twice during 1992; first in April, when to the astonishment of all the commentators and press the Tory Government, led

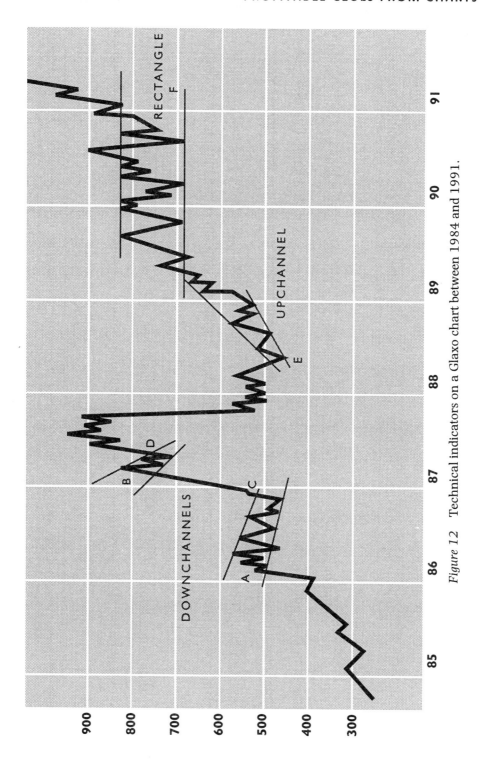

Figure 12   Technical indicators on a Glaxo chart between 1984 and 1991.

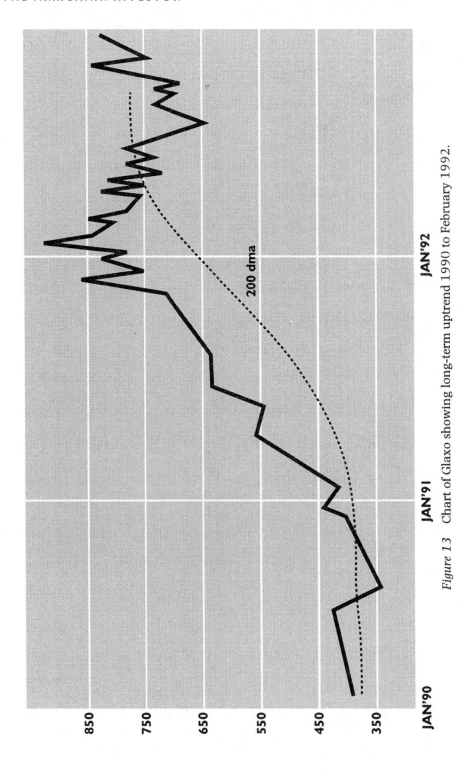

Figure 13   Chart of Glaxo showing long-term uptrend 1990 to February 1992.

by John Major, scraped back into office for a third term with a reduced majority. The markets had gloomily predicted a Labour victory, with all its doom-laden implications for higher taxes, increased public spending and rising Government intervention. With the Tories returned to power, the markets zoomed up. The FT-SE 100 index rose over 100 points on the day; this began a strong three-month trend. Smart investors who realized the privatized, partly-paid utility shares would rapidly rise after this unpredicted result were well placed to make bumper profits. Sadly, I was still a greenhorn, and was not among them.

Expect the unexpected, and the market will still surprise you.

CURRENCY TURMOIL

The second occasion in 1992 for an unpredicted outcome that produced a huge new up-trend in the market was the fiasco of sterling's forced expulsion from the exchange rate mechanism of the European Monetary System on 16 September. By releasing Britain from the deflationary impact of high German interest rates, this celebratory day was promptly dubbed 'White Wednesday'. It heralded the prospect of reflation for Britain, to reduce unemployment and increase economic activity through lower interest rates. Investors greeted this event with instant relief and so began the launch of a powerful, sixteen-month bull market.

Without any major news or random events, buyers and sellers can easily balance each other out, creating a lacklustre market. Prices move in a narrow trading range. In these structureless phases, making profits from share price movements is difficult as the market's future direction is unclear. If unexpected bad news arrives, plunging prices could result. Making new investments at these times carries more risk.

While random events can disturb the markets, a vast amount of new data is clustered, or non-random. For companies, there are interim and annual results, plus annual general meetings. Routine national news items include clustered (non-random) data on a wide range of government statistics: monthly GDP, trade figures, money supply, government borrowing, inflation, unemployment, etc. A regular diet of data drives the market. The response to sudden adverse or favourable data clusters can be a huge surge, with a rush of selling or buying.

Be prepared to wait patiently for the best investment opportunities. They crop up regularly, for those smart enough to recognize them.

WATCH THOSE TRENDS

A forming trend is easily spotted on a chart of a share or index. Moving averages give clear signals; golden crosses for buy, dead crosses for sell, or three averages marching up one behind the other in an up-trend (or down in a down-trend). Moving averages help identify times when profitable trends emerge, get established, overshoot and look ready for a serious setback or even a sharp collapse. The overshoot in a bull trend can produce enough instability to veer the market towards an unstable top, followed by a steep decline.

However, in the later stages of a boom, it is still possible to make good profits in the rising market. Knowing when to withdraw with them intact is the clever trick that separates canny investors from the late arrivals. Spotting the telltale signs at the top is not as difficult as you might think, since most of the warning signals on each occasion are fairly similar, as we shall see in Chapter 6.

VOLUME INDICATORS

Another useful indicator linked to trend formation is volume. In the UK, information on volumes traded for small company shares is not easily available. But for most larger companies, a price movement is more significant if it is accompanied by high volume (i.e. high market turnover). The rule is the volume follows the direction of the trend and a high volume in a rising market indicates that the market could move further in the same direction: the volume must confirm the trend. A high volume on rises indicates the strength of participation; more buyers encourage more buying. A big rise in volume often follows a breakout from a trading range. High volume after the breakout reinforces the signal. Paradoxically, breakouts in thin volume are good signals for a further price rise. The best trading days often occur in the thin markets before public holidays, such as between Christmas and the New Year.

Volume follows the direction of the trend.

GAPS AS STRUCTURE

It sounds odd to say gaps have structure, but as a technical factor the emergence of gaps is yet another key pointer that gives clear signals. A gap is a price interval in which no trading occurs. There is a buyer/seller vacuum and the price leaps either up or down on absolutely no turnover (volume). It occurs when market-makers move a price in response to a news item to protect their trading positions. In a rising market the gap is extremely bullish. It means the buyers have completely overwhelmed sellers. A very strong surge often results, shooting the price rapidly higher. Jesse Livermore, the canny 1920s speculator, was adept at spotting profitable trading chances created by gaps, because *a gap signals no resistance.* This is a strong sign, implying the sellers are in retreat.

A powerful combination is a gap arising on a breakout from a congestion (drifting) area. The gap indicates no resistance, and so confirms that the breakout is genuine and an up-trend can rapidly develop. This combination occurred in the UK market in April 1992, with the surprise Conservative election result (see Figure 14).

If buying momentum remains strong, more continuation gaps may appear, signalling the move may continue for as long as it has previously run so far. One final gap to note is the exhaustion gap. As its name implies, it emerges as a trend runs out of upward momentum. It stems from a spirited acceleration in the preceding rise and is confirmed if the gap is soon closed, by a falling price. Exhaustion gaps are more common in bull than bear markets. They come at the end of a long trend, with one final push of a

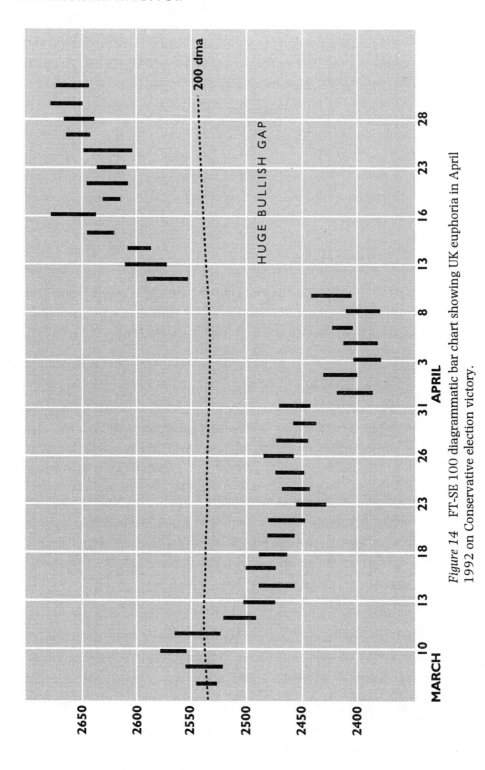

Figure 14 FT-SE 100 diagrammatic bar chart showing UK euphoria in April 1992 on Conservative election victory.

strong buying surge, before it goes into reverse as an equally strong selling surge.

PROFITING FROM BREAKOUTS

We discussed breakouts in connection with ambiguous congestion areas like base-building and rectangles. An upwards breakout is a price move out of a congestion area. It takes the price up into new territory, or up out of an earlier declining trend. A strong breakout, confirmed by high volume, is one of the most profitable investment profiles. It works equally for a market index, for a major company or for a tiny company with an illiquid market in its shares, and signals the strength of buying over selling. Sometimes, a pull back occurs to the previous congestion zone, as patient investors, nursing losses for months or years before the breakout came, rush to sell finally with a profit. The next up-thrust is even stronger, as resistance from stale sellers has disappeared and the up-thrust gains new momentum as it rises. Figures 15 to 16 show charts with some of these key features marked, including gaps and breakouts.

BUYING ON THE BREAKOUT

William O'Neil suggests you should not buy a share that has already risen 8 per cent above its breakout level, as this may have eaten too far into its profit potential. However, false breakouts do occur, and that is why I consider the fundamental picture is equally as important as the chart. If you have chosen a share which you think can double in price over a two- to three-year period, it will not matter too much if you buy on a breakout which soon aborts. You can hold on, hoping that the price will soon perform a real breakout.

Cautious investors might want to use extra indicators, to avoid buying on a false breakout. You can decide to wait for the *price to close above the breakout price on two consecutive days before buying.* If you are hesitant, take William O'Neil's advice and wait for the price to rise at least 2 per cent above the breakout price.

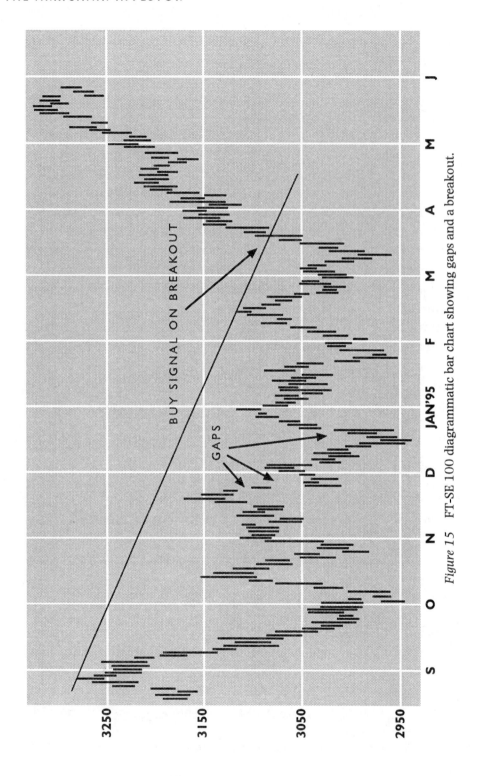

Figure 15   FT-SE 100 diagrammatic bar chart showing gaps and a breakout.

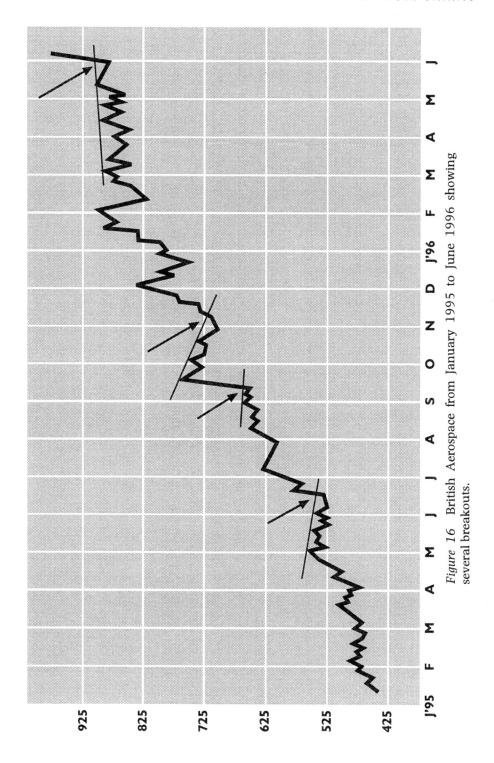

Figure 16 British Aerospace from January 1995 to June 1996 showing several breakouts.

There are plenty of rules to help you profit from your investments; the question is, will you follow those rules?

EXAGGERATED EXPECTATIONS

'Blue sky' shares with huge future expectations but small current profit streams often show incredible rises, as the price/earnings ratio explodes to the 30s, 40s, even 50s, in anticipation of a profitable story soon coming to fruition. These are 'Unipalm' stories. But they can be highly risky as it is impossible accurately to gauge a stream of future profits in companies making large start-up losses. The whole plan may go horribly wrong and end in disaster, but understanding how such stories unfold means in the early stages we can make good profits, while watching the technical indicators for evidence of an unfavourable change. My investment in Unipalm, the small Internet provider; gives an indication of how to use FASTER GAINS for evaluating shares in companies with no profitable current earnings.

THE UNIPALM STORY

True to form, we were away on a week's short break in Spain in May 1995 when Unipalm's broker issued a note on the excellent progress it was making in building its client base. At its March 1994 flotation at 100p, the Internet subsidiary was achieving an order intake of about £100,000 new annual subscription business per month. By November 1994, this had reached £390,000, with 34 new corporate subscribers. The initial aim was an order intake of £600,000 per month within two years from flotation. But new business was running so far ahead of target for the group that by March 1995, new order intake had reached £750,000 a month and it had in excess of 600 customers.

This tremendous news boosted the share price so that it doubled in a month. On returning from holiday I caught up with this story and checked Unipalm with FASTER GAINS. On the essential fundamental facts, all the performance on earnings per share and the long-term growth of those earnings were unfulfilled promises which might or might never be realized. Following the flotation, Unipalm had plenty of cash but was making only very slender profits.

FUNDAMENTAL FACTORS

Unipalm was a very small company, and the supply/demand situation on the shares made large swings possible because the directors held 25 per cent and institutions held another 43 per cent of the 20.6 million shares. This meant only 32 per cent of the shares were free in the market. There was certainly a *big* 'something-new' element in the story, as everything linked to the Internet and providing services to it was hot news during the American technology boom of 1995.

BUY SIGNALS ON THE CHART

However, with technical analysis, Unipalm's chart was giving several strong buy signals. Listing them here, the favourable signs included:

i   The long-term base it had been building at a price of 125p. This phase stretched over about six months, as shown in Figure 17.

ii All the three moving averages, the short 20-day, the medium 50-day and the long-term 200-day averages, were bunched close together. When this occurs it is again a very positive position.

iii During May, the share price had leapt up a full 100 per cent in a few days. This represented a most powerful breakout signal from the lengthy 125p base.

iv Although volume figures are not easily obtainable on very small shares such as Unipalm, the chart showed there had been several days of higher than usual volume during April and May.

v   As for stock market direction, by the spring of 1995, the stock market was beginning a big upward surge, which offered a favourable background for a new investment in shares.

Unipalm is definitely on the fringes of the FASTER GAINS formula, as the fundamentals are uncertain in the early stages of its development, but I liked the story, I was very impressed by the chart buy signals, and I thought the shares would perform well.

PATIENT TRACKING FOR UNIPALM

I decided to track the share, hoping that after the doubling leap upwards, profit-taking would pull the price down from the 250p peak. The drop took over six weeks, but by the end of June the price had fallen to 187p. As you can see from the chart, Unipalm only spent one night's close at this level before it shot straight up to about 212p.

I like to buy a share as it bounces off a low point. At L on the chart, the price of Unipalm shares had just dipped below both the 20-day and 50-day moving averages. There was always the possibility that the price would plunge down towards 125p again, to meet up with the 200-day moving average slowly rising to around 135p at M, before it made any new upward moves. It is therefore best to wait to see if the price will fall further or move back up from this point L. Buying small shares at the price you have pre-planned can be extremely difficult because when they move the action can be very rapid. On 29 June I was not able to buy at my chosen price of 195p as the price moved up away from me too quickly.

ACTION TIME ON UNIPALM

I bought 1,429 Unipalm shares at 203p as the price began ticking up quickly on 29 June from the 187p low. The cost inside the Single Company PEP was £2,966.00. News items about Unipalm's continuing good progress, crowned by the announcement that it was in talks on a possible takeover, shot the price up to 400p by mid-August. I sold 429 shares at 400p and the other 1,000 at

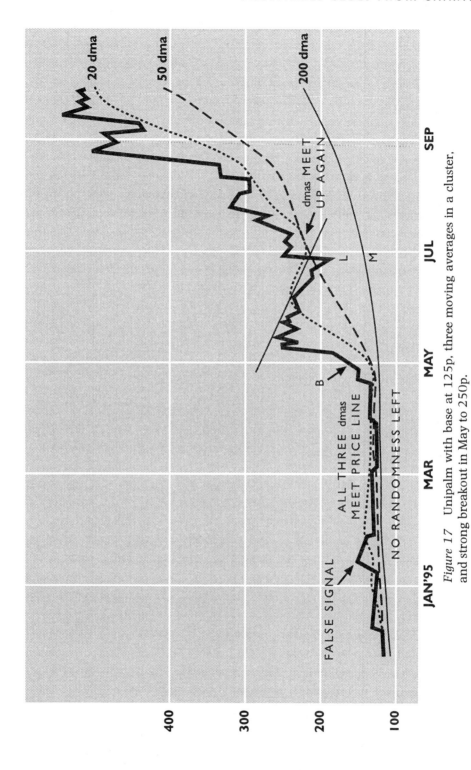

Figure 17 Unipalm with base at 125p, three moving averages in a cluster, and strong breakout in May to 250p.

425p to build the original £2,966 into £5,972 within seven weeks. This was a gain of £3,006, or 101 per cent. Trying to repeat this performance may prove difficult.

FANTASTIC FLAGS

One of the most exciting chart formations with huge profit potential is a flag. It is a short-term counter-reaction (for profit-taking) in an aggressive up-trend. A sudden rapid run-up on large volume in response to exceptionally good news will often be followed by a pause of two to three weeks, during which time the moving averages catch up with the great upward share price spurt. This may dip slightly with some profit-taking, but if, after a pause, the price rises back to the first high point, the chances are good that it may continue rushing up, to duplicate the initial rise.

Measuring from the breakout to the first high point as a percentage gives an indication as to where the second great leap up may take the price. Flag formations are clearly seen in charts for Superscape, Chiroscience and WPP, shown in Figures 18 to 20.

The flag is another stunning display of market structure.

A flag formation is another example of heavy buying (or selling). The first strong upward move occurs with large volume, and perhaps, a gap up. Then comes a short profit-taking pause, before another rapid rush up in the price. This may be associated with institutional buying or an important news announcement or some other key fundamental event.

PATTERNS THAT FAIL

Unfortunately, we must note a cautionary warning when making important investment decisions. Sometimes, the patterns fail to follow through to the expected conclusion. But that should be no surprise as the markets are unpredictable, which is why I prefer to concentrate more on those patterns that show unambiguous structure.

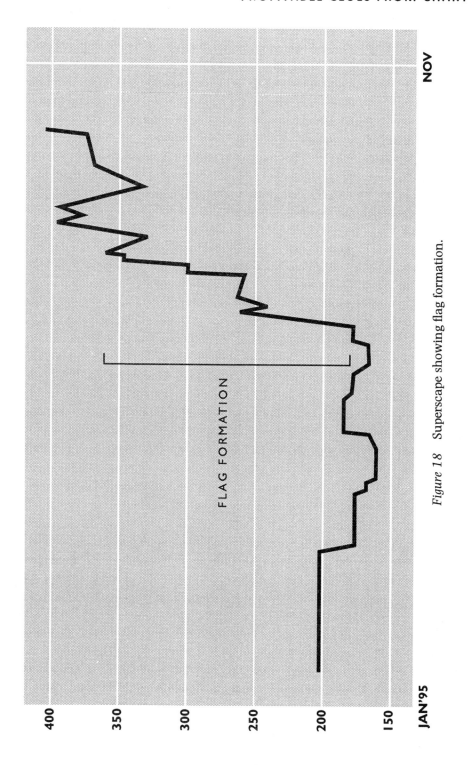

Figure 18 Superscape showing flag formation.

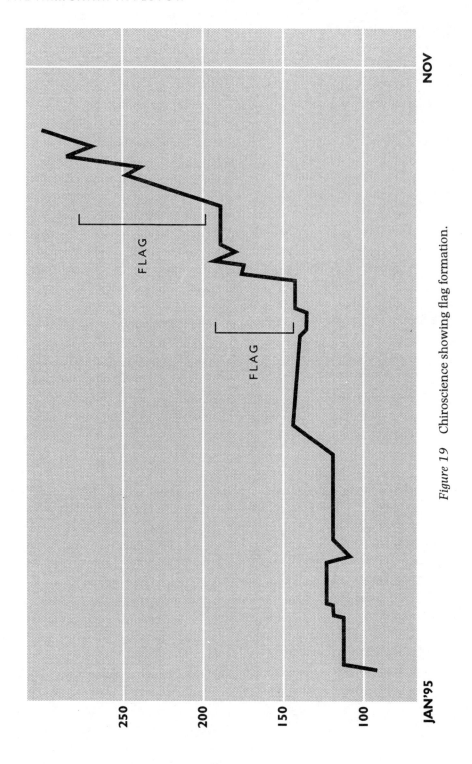

Figure 19   Chiroscience showing flag formation.

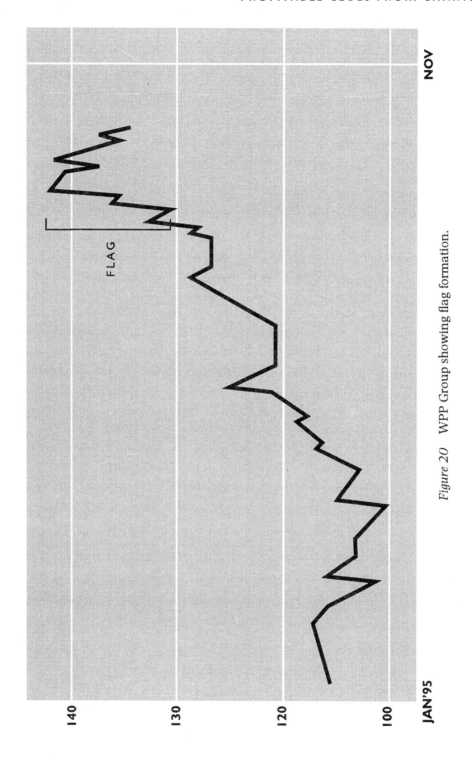

Figure 20 WPP Group showing flag formation.

*No one indicator is conclusive. They work best
when used in groups.*

The best buy and sell signals arise from confirmatory indications in more than one area of technical analysis: from chart patterns, moving averages, volumes, trend formations. We have seen throughout the chapter how these can be used. However, on many occasions, chart patterns fail. They do not proceed to their expected completion.

To take advantage of the structures beneath the random shock events to which all markets are prone, we must concentrate on those situations that offer the best potential rewards with the lowest level of risk. As we have seen, technical tools that help us to reveal and study the structure of the market will also help us to identify these highly profitable phases. While this represents a small part of the market's overall dynamics, these more predictable periods can be used to make a lot of money. Chart patterns, moving averages, trend formations, news-driven events, are all examples of structure-illuminating features which help to separate the strong decisive movements from the lengthy phases of idle drift when it is far more risky and unprofitable to be heavily invested.

If you simply concentrate on catching the major bull market moves and sitting idly on the sidelines in the downturns, your profits would accumulate without involving a prodigious effort. This is a difficult trick to perform, so 'steady as she goes' is perhaps a safer route for novices.

However, trends appear in market indices as well as in the charts of individual shares. It definitely pays handsomely to watch out for the trends. When a trend develops, the market has become orderly, more predictable, more highly structured. And infinitely more useful to armchair investors hoping to make large profits.

*When greedy people rush to buy shares at the top of the
market, you should be delighted to sell your shares
to them.*

CHAPTER 5

The riskless paper chase to profits

Focus your attention on opportunities that offer the greatest chance of success.

It seems a bit back-to-front to discuss planning a paper portfolio when you are now halfway through a book designed to give novice investors a hands-on guide to investment success. However, you must have a clear grasp of what you want to achieve – your goals, and how you are going to achieve them, your detailed plans – before you can set about putting your plan into action. You must also have a reasonable idea of what is involved in building a successful investment system. Having covered several aspects of this now, compiling and running a paper portfolio is an excellent trial and error routine to get you started, while you read the last four chapters which deal with tracking the market and running your action plan.

In this chapter we shall consider the basic essentials of running a portfolio by using a paper prototype. While your paper investments are actually in place, you can concentrate on improving your investment skills, ready to embark on the real thing. At the same time, one of the most important lessons to grasp is how to manage risk properly. If you can do that, the chances of losing your hard-earned cash will diminish and so will your fears about investing for real.

TRIAL AND ERROR ROUTINES

Finding a stock-picking routine that suits your investment temperament may take time, especially if, at the outset, you haven't got the faintest notion of what your basic attitudes to investment really are. This is not a problem. As with any new skill, trial and error is an essential part of the learning process. I tried several different stock-picking routines until I settled on FASTER GAINS by reading how the successful gurus had made their money. I knew FASTER GAINS was right for me when I saw I was making more successful investment choices than faulty ones. The profits began building and I felt happy with the portfolio of shares I was holding. These are all positive signs that the investment story is on track. In short, when you start picking more winners than losers, and when you feel less anxious about holding your portfolio, you know you are making progress. In essence, your investment pot is growing in value as your skills improve.

It is a radiant experience when your research brings handsome gains in the shares you have bought.

Trial-and-error routines are extremely useful for beginners. I used them constantly; for choosing a broker I was happy with, for deciding on the newsletters that suited me best and, of course, for stock-picking routines. You can use a trial-and-error approach for any of these areas and even for experimenting with a paper portfolio while you pluck up the courage to enter the real market.

PAPER PROOF
....

One approach that could be helpful would be to start running a paper portfolio as soon as you have read the stock-picking chapters in this book. Then you can watch the progress of your paper investments while you are reading how to set up a good tailor-made investment system. By the time all the building blocks of your overall plan are in place, you should have a better idea of how to run your portfolio and can judge how good your initial choices were that you made early on before your knowledge had expanded through the reading and learning process.

As an exercise for learning what to do and how to do it, running a paper portfolio can be highly instructive. Whatever the outcome, you should feel happy. If you make losses, you feel happy that this is just a dummy run and you can learn painlessly to do things better. If you make paper gains, you should also be very happy. Never mind that it is not real money in the bank. Being right is the greatest boost to confidence I have yet discovered. It should give you the courage to ensure you can go on making profits when you invest for real.

All the lessons you learn are important, but one key point to grasp is that there is absolutely no shortage of worthwhile opportunities. There will be endless occasions for making profits. They crop up almost every month of the year. This is one of the most exciting aspects of learning how to invest for profits. You can almost always find a profitable situation, once you know what to look for, where to find it, and how to reduce the risk of it going wrong once you have made a purchase.

Another use for the trial-and-error approach when you are just beginning is to run a small test portfolio with your first purchases. If you buy just one or two small holdings, you can monitor their progress over a period of about six months and then assess the results. You can be looking out for other suitable shares to buy while you are waiting to judge the performance of your first two. You should be willing to change to another stock-picking routine after six months if you feel uncomfortable with the one you are using. This is especially so if you feel your results could be improved. Turn to another stock-picking routine and run another six-month test.

> *There are endless opportunities to make profits*
> *in rising markets.*

A PAPER PORTFOLIO FOR BEGINNERS

When you are learning about companies, it is extremely helpful to read the London Stock Market Report on the very back page of the 'Companies and Markets' section of the daily *Financial Times* or whichever financial newspaper you buy. The reports give news on what the brokers and analysts are recommending to their big professional City clients. Often they advise clients to sell or avoid a share, noting their reasons. The report will also show you which shares are in fashion, which are unpopular and what the broad trends of the market itself are. Is it rising, falling or drifting? This part of the paper is extremely informative and even if time is short you should make a point of reading it as often as you can, daily if possible.

At the outset, you may already have a few favourite companies you would like to follow more closely, by 'buying' them for your newly established paper portfolio. But if you do not have any pet companies you would like to monitor in this way, simply take three large blue chip UK companies that catch your eye from one issue of the London Stock Market Report, to get you started. The way you choose them is not important, but it is fun to select some that have received strong backing from three different major broking houses, such as Barclays de Zoete Wedd, SBC Warburg and NatWest Securities, so you can see how their recommendations work out in practice. Or you may notice some companies which have shown a recent rise in price or been prominent in the news for takeovers, management changes or achieving large new contracts. Each of the three should preferably come from different sectors of the market: food retailers, oil companies, pharmaceuticals, banks, etc. You might even like to judge which of these sectors you think will do well over the next few months. The back page of the Saturday *FT* lists the best and worst sectors for the year to date under the caption 'FT-SE-A Indices – Leaders & Laggards'.

The companies featured in the Stock Market Report will usually include some smaller companies as well as the very largest UK businesses. You should concentrate on these major companies for this test, as picking successful small growth shares is much more difficult for outright beginners. If your first blue chip paper portfolio works well, you can start a second one for the small companies you select with FASTER GAINS, again running the trial for about six months. Focus first on the giants of the UK quoted companies, familiar names like Sainsbury, Glaxo Wellcome, Shell, Marks and Spencer. Do not worry unduly about calculating the purchase costs, if you cannot sort these out. Divide your paper cash into three main chunks and 'buy' 100 or 1,000 shares in three companies which most appeal or catch your eye.

On a blank sheet of paper, enter the date of your purchase, the price you paid (the mid-price quoted in the newspaper) and the total cost. Choose three shares which feature in the top 100 UK quoted companies, meaning they will all be constituents of the FT-SE 100 index. For the purpose of this experiment, it will not matter greatly if one or two of your choices are not actually FT-SE 100 shares. Allow room to record the level of the FT-SE 100 index on the day you made your purchases and leave spaces along the page to record, once a week, the closing prices of your three chosen shares plus the FT-SE 100 index, usually using Friday evening's closing prices. Monitor how they do for about three months, to get a flavour of what is going on and how to set about building your own portfolio.

A blue chip is a gambling counter. But if you gamble with your hard-earned investment capital, you may lose the bet.

At the end of your experiment calculate the actual and the percentage rise or fall of each share from the day you began and compare that with the rise or fall of the FT-SE 100. *This is not a recommended way to choose a real portfolio*; but as a beginner's trial run, it gives a feel for how prices change. You may notice that during the few days after you begin, broker recommended shares show handsome rises, following these experts' endorsement. Many fund managers receive this advice the day before it appears in the *FT* Report, so you can climb on board, using real expert advice, to see how it works out in practice.

A seven-week illustration is shown on page 106. I chose three

---

BLUE CHIP PAPER PORTFOLIO

Date	Shares Chosen	Reason
11/8/95	Asda	Best performing FT-SE share
11/8/95	Carlton Comm.	Strong media sector
11/8/95	Vodaphone	Plenty of buying interest

Paper Portfolio Details

Share	Number	Mid Price (p)	Cost (£)
ASDA	100	106.25	106.25
CCM	10	1074.00	107.40
VOD	100	261.50	261.50
		Total Cost	£475.15

Weekly Record of Paper Portfolio

Share	Dates 11/8	18/8	25/8	2/9	8/9	16/9	22/9	29/9
FT-SE100	3467.50	3509.80	3524.90	3509.40	3554.50	3564.60	3514.80	3508.20
ASDA	106.25	103.25	103.50	109.00	107.25	106.50	101.75	103.50
CCM	1074.00	1075.00	1067.00	1043.00	1068.00	1058.00	1022.00	1035.00
VOD	261.50	276.00	269.00	272.00	272.00	279.50	265.50	265.50

[Value on 29 September 1995: £472.50]

---

shares, based on good buying support for 11 August 1995, the day my example trial began. It certainly was not a long enough test to show any clear moves. However, 13 September was a market peak, so buying on 11 August was far too late to put the portfolio securely into profits before prices fell during September.

Face up to the fear of making losses by getting to know the facts.

Although this was a very short experiment period, it shows how quickly prices can diverge from a starting position. Over this seven-week test, only the FT-SE 100 and Vodaphone rose, while both Asda and Carlton Communications fell. The FT-SE 100 rose by 1.2 per cent; Vodaphone rose by 1.5 per cent; Asda fell by 2.9 per cent; Carlton Communications lost 3.6 per cent. Out of curiosity, I rechecked all these prices on 24 February 1996, to see how different they were for a full, six-month period, and again on 29 August 1996 when the paper portfolio had been running for a full year.

	24/2/96	% Rise
FT-SE 100	3752.7	8.2
ASDA	104.5	-1.6
CCM	1019.0	-5.1
VOD	235	-10.1

Value on 24 February 1996: £441.40
Loss: £33.75, i.e. 7%

	29/8/96	% Rise
FT-SE 100	3918.7	13.0
ASDA	113.5	6.7
CCM	486.5*	-9.4
VOD	248.5	-5.0

Value on 29 August 1996: £459.3
Loss: £15.85, i.e. 3.3%

*prior to share split price would
have been 973p (486.5 x 2)

These surprise results show how difficult it can be to make money on your investments if you literally 'take-your-pick' without having a sound investment plan to work to. Over a six-month period when the FT-SE 100 index rose 8.2 per cent, the value of my blue chip portfolio had fallen by 7 per cent. Out of interest, I looked back to see how my real portfolio growth compared with the trial run. I only had one FT-SE 100 shareholding of 906 British Aerospace plus 1,750 British Aerospace warrants (giving me the right to buy the shares at 525p on certain future dates). I also had a wide range of small company shares in many different sectors. At 22 February, the nearest date for which I had a total value, my portfolio had increased by 25 per cent, against the FT-SE-A All-Share, broadly based index rise of 8.3 per cent. The following week was even more successful for my portfolio, giving an overall rise of 29 per cent from 11 August 1995 start date to 1 March 1996.

This result demonstrates the value of carefully planned investing but it also shows how a casual stock-picking routine can actually produce negative results over a six-month period. Not one of my FT–SE 100 paper selections was showing a positive gain in February 1996, whereas the British Aerospace shares I bought on 18 September 1995 had risen from 709p to 852p, a rise of 20 per cent, and the warrants, bought on 10 October 1995 at 263p had risen to 364p, a rise of 38 per cent.

By 29 August 1996 the FT-SE 100 had hit a record all-time high of 3,918.7, a 12-month rise of 13 per cent. But on 29 August the three shares in the paper portfolio showed the following prices:– Asda: $113\frac{1}{2}$p (a 12-month rise of 6.7 per cent), Carlton Communications: $486\frac{1}{2}$p [after a 2-for-1 share split] (a 12-month fall of 9.4 per cent) and Vodaphone: $248\frac{1}{2}$p (a 12-month fall of 5 per cent).

The portfolio loss was now 3.3 per cent after 1 year while the FT-SE 100 had risen 13 per cent over that period.

There are plenty of ways to reduce risk once you start to prepare properly before investing.

MANAGING RISK

Quite unintentionally, my paper portfolio has highlighted one of the novice's greatest investment fears, the risk of losing money. By simply taking an off-the-cuff attitude to share selection, you run a very real risk of making losses rather than gains. By giving comparative figures for my carefully chosen, and constantly monitored portfolio, I hope to have demonstrated that my skills with my well-established investment system far outweigh my abilities as a random, anything-goes share-picker.

So what do we actually mean when we talk about risk? To me the notion of risk suggests two things: first, exposure to danger, and second the possibility of losses. When we are investing in the market, we have to safeguard our capital from serious loss by tipping the odds as much in our favour as we possibly can. There are several ways that this can be achieved. Each one forms an important part of your overall risk management approach.

Increasing your knowledge is one of the best ways of reducing risk.

UNDERSTANDING RISK CONTROL

Getting to grips with risk control is a tricky part of your investment tactics. One good way to begin is to read the investment books written by or about the most successful investors. These accounts invariably include details of how they control risk. They often relate experiences of horrendous losses in their novice days, when they failed to understand how to manage the risks. You can cut out a lot of aggravation and expense by riding up the learning curve on their coat-tails.

The experience of investment gurus is a wonderful source of inspiration. It will stimulate you to prepare your own investment system. This essential step is itself a crucial element in reducing risk, because it is your blueprint plan. Anything that prepares you better for taking actions, also helps crystallize your plans for avoiding the worst possible scenario, if things go wrong.

Another way to minimize risk is to be prepared to stay flexible. If things are not going well, you should be willing to revise your whole investment scheme, even if it means starting from scratch. Better still, go back to your paper portfolio trials. Try not to continue blindly running your portfolio if you find you are consistently losing money. On the other hand, if circumstances look favourable, and you are making real profits, be ready to modify your plans to take advantage of these new conditions. The market is forever springing surprises upon us, so it will be a big disadvantage if you become too rigid in your thinking and planning.

PRACTISE RISK CONTROL

The first stepping stone to controlling the risks is to devise a short set of rules that suit your investment routine. Do not worry if you are unsure at the outset what your rules should be. In your reading, you will find that the gurus make frequent mention of the rules they think are extremely important. So you could start with a short list of their collective rules. Having a set of rules helps to reduce the risk of making large losses if your plans go wrong. Start with a few basic rules that seem to cover your immediate requirements. Write them down and try not to change them too often. Review them once every month to begin with, but as your experience grows you may not need to change them more than once every six months or a year.

OBEY YOUR RULES

To start you thinking, here is a brief list of suggested rules you may like to consider. A list of about ten is the most you should need.

i   *Always obey the rules of your own system.* This enforces good self-control

ii *Don't change your rules unless you first do a full review* of your recent investment performance, say once a month to start with, then every six months, and at least once every year.

iii *Make regular reviews of your progress*, to ensure you are still on track to achieve your targets.

iv *Be ready to examine your mistakes and learn from them.* This is hard to do, as being wrong is a dent to your self-esteem so sweeping mistakes aside is an easier option, but then you will not learn how to avoid repeating them.

You need never make the same mistake twice –
when there are so many others you can try.

v   *Never make impulse buys.* This is one of the most sensible rules and also the one most easily broken. My trial paper portfolio was based on 'hunches' about the three FT-SE 100 shares I chose, and after six months it was not looking very encouraging.

vi   *Don't take tips from other people.* They may bring nothing but aggravation.

vii *Always weigh up the pros and cons of each investment choice.* This means looking at the worst possible scenario in case things go wrong.

viii *Be willing to wait patiently for the exceptional opportunities to arrive.*

ix   *Run profits slowly and cut losses quickly.*

x   *Always calculate the risks to minimize the losses.*

Something you know very well is rarely a cause for fear.

CALCULATE THE RISKS

You can select the lowest risk investment by assessing the advantages and disadvantages of each share you are considering as an investment. This involves exploring all the avenues of stock-picking information, including the fundamental facts, the chart appearance, the future prospects for the company and the current state of the market. From the fundamental facts about a company and its chart pattern, you can work out a suitable buying price and a possible target price. You can also work out the possible profit versus the size of the possible losses, if you assume the share price could move between two estimated values. For example, suppose the shares for Widgets Group are priced at 100p and your target price is 200p, but the chart suggests it might fall back to 70p. The profit scenario is +100 per cent, but the loss at 70p would be −30 per cent. If the figures work out like that, you might decide simply to watch the share and wait until it gets closer to 70p. If you buy it at 80p, the sums work out completely differently. Now the profit percentage if it reaches 200p is +150 per cent, while the estimated loss on a fall to 70p is −12.5 per cent. It may sound complicated, but examples were discussed in Chapter 2 on stock-picking, and Chapter 4 on using charts.

The best reason for practising risk control is to avoid the chance of making large losses. There are several ways to achieve this. You must try to cut losses fast, by setting a price at which you will sell, if the price moves against you after you buy a share. Unless you are convinced the story is rock solid when you buy, you should stick firmly to your selling price to avoid running up big losses. In the case of Widgets Group, by waiting until the price fell back to 80p before buying, we reduced the possible loss from 30 to 12.5 per cent. But suppose you bought 1,000 Widgets Group shares at 80p and three days later they hit 68p; what would you do? This is not a trick question; it can happen as soon as you buy your first share. Before adding in the costs of buying and selling, you are showing a 15 per cent loss.

The sensible route is to review quickly your calculations, to ensure you were right about your target price of 200p. Then consider whether there is a special reason for the fall. Has there been a profits warning? Has a director sold a large block of shares? Did an institution sell part of its holding? Has there been an unfavourable announcement from the company? Did the company announce results, which led to some profit-taking? Is the whole market falling? Next look again at the chart, to decide where the price might settle. You might decide to sell at 68p, if you feel a 15 per cent loss is too high. If you decide to hold on, then set another selling target and act firmly on it if the price falls down to hit it.

If I am unsure, I invariably sell and watch again from the sidelines. Many observers think this is a foolhardy way to invest. They reason that if you are in for the long term, you should ignore short-term fluctuations. I think differently. I have only a small capital sum. I always think about the lost opportunities passing me by while I sit nursing a losing position hoping it will eventually come right. I bought shares in Kleinwort Benson's European Privatization investment trust in the January 1994 launch, but soon realized a big downturn had arrived. I sold, taking a 20 per cent loss, so I could reinvest the rest to recoup it. As we saw in Chapter 1, investors who held on are still waiting to see a positive return from this investment trust.

The second reason given for not selling too often is that it clocks up extra commissions for the broker. This is the logic of the mad house. My top priority for investing in the stock market is to make good profits. If I have made a poor share selection, should I be thinking about not handing the broker two additional commissions, one when I sell and a second when I reinvest, or should I be worrying about choosing a better investment to buy? To me, the choice is very clear-cut. I do not begrudge the broker his commission, but I do not allow those considerations to interfere with my decisions on selling poor performers quickly and trying to hold on to the winners.

It is better to sell a share that is not behaving as you planned. You can always buy it back again later.

PORTFOLIO PLANNING

Another method of reducing risk is to ensure each of your shareholdings is in a different market sector. It would be folly to buy shares in Tesco, Sainsbury and Asda, for example, in case the whole food retailing sector fell for some reason. It is obviously better to spread the holdings among many different sectors, so that the risk of one suddenly collapsing will not greatly affect your portfolio.

Another central way of controlling risk is to plan your portfolio carefully. This means deciding on the numbers of shares to hold and how much money to invest in each choice. If you begin with £20,000, you could split that into five holdings of roughly £3,750 with a cash float of £1,250. If the market is drifting or unsettled, hold more cash, say £4,000 or 20 per cent. To find £4,000 in cash, you can either sell one holding outright, or reduce the sizes of two or three holdings. If you feel very optimistic, you can be fully invested, while watching events, in case the market takes a downward turn.

If you do not have *at least £10,000* to start with, I think you should begin by building your unit trust portfolio, either with regular savings plans, or with small lump sums, until you have saved enough to invest directly in shares. We will return to ideas behind risk control again in Chapter 8 when we discuss routines for monitoring the portfolio.

> **Trying to catch the top or bottom of the market is a high-risk strategy. It is very difficult to time the top or bottom, so the losses can soon mount up.**

ADD SOME PEP

If you are going to start saving through small regular contributions, using the PEP route is ideal. Early in your investment planning you will want to consider how you are going to build up your future nest egg. One of the most successful routes now available is through regular savings in tax-free Personal Equity Plans (PEPs). Perhaps one of the greatest boons from PEPs is the lack of paperwork because there is no need to keep detailed records for the Inland Revenue. As there is absolutely no tax to pay, you get gross dividends, capital gains without deductions for tax and gross interest on cash balances held within the PEP. Jim Slater, in *PEP Up Your Wealth*, advocates the O'Higgins system for making sizeable profits within a PEP by using high yield share selections. By investing in out-of-favour blue chip companies with relatively high dividend payments, you can afford to wait for them to come back into favour. When that happens, you will make profits from the rise in the share price, in addition to the large dividends you receive.

My big investment idea was to use FASTER GAINS to build the PEPs up as quickly and substantially as I could using high growth shares to build up the capital and virtually ignoring the yield or dividends earned. I found this was extremely difficult to do in practice. I have only succeeded three times in achieving what I am trying to do. First, there was my investment in Glaxo shares, held in a PEP from September 1990 to January 1992. My second great PEP gain came from my investment in Unipalm, the small Internet provider, described in Chapter 4, to illustrate what I have been trying to achieve by using FASTER GAINS for growing large PEPs. The third gain was with Sage, covered in Chapter 9.

The arrival of PEPs is tremendous news for armchair investors.

PEP-FULL OF IDEAS

For serious long-term investors, the arrival of PEPs is wonderful news. PEP investing is a superb way to generate real wealth. By summer 1996 investors who had taken advantage of the full PEP allowance (currently £9,000 per person each year), would have built up a fund of around £73,000 per person since their introduction in 1987. For a married couple the total would be double at £146,000, and this is only the initial investments. It excludes any gains (and ignores any losses) and reinvested dividends plus gross interest on the cash balances.

I have not taken full advantage of the permitted allowances. My idea for growing a PEP fund is to put all my PEP eggs in one basket. I use just one very efficient execution-only PEP fund manager and concentrate on self-select general PEPs (as opposed to the smaller Single Company PEPs), where I can choose the shares I want to hold from almost every size of share in the main stock market list. And I add the full allowance each year (currently £6,000) to increase the overall size of the fund. That way I have only two accounts to worry about, one for myself and the other for my husband. As the two funds grow, I can buy larger shareholdings and benefit from the reduced commission charges. If I opened a new fund for only £6,000 each year, I would have considerably less flexibility in handling several small sums than I can gain dealing with one larger fund. I also have power of attorney to run my husband's PEP, which is a great help in a partnership where only one partner wants the bother of monitoring the portfolios.

There are several other important points to act as guidelines for building a PEP nest egg. You should try if possible to add your full entitlement each year. If you cannot afford a lump sum investment, add to your plan with regular payments on a monthly or quarterly basis. Unless you have a very large capital base I should leave the Single Company PEPs alone, as these have different rules and are an extra inconvenience as they each have to be managed as separate accounts. Each Single Company PEP is a separate entity. You cannot add to it in the following year, as you can with general PEPs. I find this extremely tiresome. The size of the general PEPs will soon mount up if you concentrate on those alone. It also helps the funds grow faster if you leave all the gross dividends and the gross interest in the PEPs, so they can be reinvested with the proceeds from your next share sale.

Avoid making any withdrawals as it can be difficult to rebuild the fund from a lower level. If cash is needed for an emergency, use money in the initial cash pool, as once PEP money is withdrawn its tax-exempt status is permanently lost. Once the fund is large enough, you may decide to switch to the O'Higgins investment scheme, as that would provide attractive dividends to be taken as tax-free income while, hopefully, the capital fund continues growing. An important advantage of PEPs is that although they lose their tax-free status on the death of the holder, the money pot is still there. This compares most favourably with pension money, which in most cases (depending on how it is initially set up) is completely or more than fifty-per cent lost when the pensioner dies.

Building up a PEP fund is one of the most versatile ways of saving for the future.

CHAPTER 6

Market watch

The market sends out a stream of signals.
The trouble is you may not know how to decode them.

Investors with a natural brilliance for stock-picking can spend a lifetime building their fortunes, without giving the state of the markets or the global economy more than a passing glance. Warren Buffett and Peter Lynch are certainly in this league. But for most of us, Jim Slater's Zulu principle is a safer guide. He suggests we concentrate on only a small area, so as to become more knowledgeable in that one sphere. Although the first priority has to be a circle of competence on your stock-picking routine, if, in addition, you learn to understand the ebbs and flows of market events, you can familiarize yourself with the key factors that move markets. This offers a greater insight into how different important events may affect your shareholdings and may help you protect your profits in a downturn.

If you have found a gem of a small company operating in a niche market that is growing fast, with a huge order book and no debt, the chances are it will stand rock solid through all the buffeting of a market drop. Or it may dip slightly, while the rest of the market falls much further. These wonder stocks are hard to find in the UK, so if you discover one, or two, the veteran's approach would be to sit with them through all the market's nerve-wracking gyrations. They may ultimately reward you by proving to be examples of Peter Lynch's famous 'ten-baggers'. If they grow ten times while you are holding them, your performance will be greatly enhanced. Conversely, these little nuggets are so highly prized by the market, that if they suffer any setback at all, the price may drop dramatically, similar to the Telspec situation mentioned previously.

Follow the story, and if it remains good, ignore the market.

However, most of the shares in your portfolio are likely to follow the direction of the market. This means that, in general, knowing about the business cycle and what makes the economy tick is useful grist to the mill of accumulating knowledge.

A SENSE OF DIRECTION

The quickest way to get lost is to set off without a map. Successful investment requires a good sense of direction and this applies to almost all investors, novices and seasoned campaigners alike. You may eventually reach a stage where you decide you have perfected your stock-picking system or taken it to a level that fulfils your goals. Or better still, you may have decided to hold your shares for the very long term. In that case, you can put your portfolio onto 'automatic pilot', monitoring it once every three months, to reassure yourself it is still on track. Then you may follow the fortunes of your shares, and be indifferent to what the general market is doing. I hope this transition will eventually arrive for me.

But most amateur investment sleuths need all the clues they can find. And that definitely includes a need to know what the market is actually doing now. Knowing that helps us to fix where we are now in the business, economic and financial cycles. As we have seen, statistics regularly show that small investors buy at a market peak and sell at the bottom. Knowing how the market behaves will eliminate some of this folly-investing. I am sure my poor early performance was due to the fact that I paid scant attention to the background market conditions when I began.

These background conditions provide useful information on how to judge what effects events in the wider world will have on the shares we hold. So first we must understand in outline how these factors work. Then we need to monitor the market to help us keep in touch with the major economic, political and financial trends.

You are likely to be wrong, and very disappointed if you think the future will be just like the past.

UNDERSTAND THE MARKET

Think of the five to ten companies in which you have invested some money; your companies belong to you and probably many thousands of other investors, including some of the directors, some institutional investors and other small private investors. There are several occasions when a company needs to come to the market, usually to raise funds, and this is facilitated if the company is publicly listed on an authorized stock market.

Suppose it needs new cash for expansion. The company may raise a bank loan, but it would have to offer security on the loan, in the form of deeds on a property or other assets, and it would have to pay interest on the debt. It may choose instead to offer new shares to its existing shareholders, often at a discount to the current price. This would be a rights issue, where existing holders have the 'right', if they so choose, to buy new shares in proportion to their existing holding, at a stated discount to the current market price. The company gets extra cash to implement its new proposals. If these are successful, the shareholders enjoy the profits of the expansion. If the plans are unsuccessful, the earnings per share figure may fall. The same amount of earnings is now being spread between a larger number of shares.

When you invest in a new issue that has just been launched, as for example in the UK Government's privatization issues, the existing owners of the company have opted for a public listing for one of many different reasons. Most companies want to take advantage of the greater publicity that comes with being a quoted company, or they want to repay debts incurred while being privately owned, or to see their shares traded more easily because there are professional market-makers willing to make a price for buyers and sellers. Some companies might hope to raise money, now or in the future, for expansion. All these activities improve a company's flexibility and range of choices, if it is operating within the orbit of an official stock market. Ultimately, its trading prospects and earnings ability will be improved.

Of course, sometimes the market does not understand a good investment idea. This is why it is possible for really smart investors to make huge profits. During the 1980s, both Richard Branson, of Virgin fame, and Sir Andrew Lloyd Webber, the composer who created a company called The Really Useful Company, found their shares were grossly misunderstood by the market. They resented the low value the Stock Exchange put on their underlying worth. And both these entrepreneurs took their shares private again, and went on to make private fortunes.

Fortunately, the market can sometimes be slow to recognize good value. Alert investors can profit from this market oversight.

EFFECTS ON COMPANIES

The companies we have invested in are one tiny group within the huge stock market, that is slowly moving through the various phases of its activity. Our companies will be affected by events that concern them specifically, including results, contract or new product announcements, takeover bids or profits warnings. But there are also internal stock market events that may affect the shares we hold, including half-days for public holidays, as occurs on Christmas Eve, when activity is low, or the summer season when institutional investors are on holiday. Then there are certain days of possible high volatility, due to special expiry dates for **traded options** or **futures contracts** that are linked to the FT-SE 100 index.

All these occasions form the 'technical' side of the way the market operates. They have virtually nothing to do with any fundamental facts that affect the value of shares but are still important factors operating on share prices. But there are several other influences that interact with this technical market scene, and they all occur at different times, making a rather confusing picture.

THE URGE TO MERGE

One important effect is created by all the other quoted companies that we do not have in our portfolio. Events in their lives can impact directly on our holdings. For example, when pharmaceuticals giant, Glaxo, a major FT-SE 100 index company, made a bid for another huge pharmaceuticals company, Wellcome, early in 1995, the market was enthusiastic, hoping other pharmaceutical companies would become the subjects of other bids. Several shares in the pharmaceuticals sector rose in tandem with Wellcome's shares, and the market was off on one of its favourite pastimes, 'hunt the next bid prospect'. If the market is in the right mood, this treasure hunt quickly spreads to other sectors. It is most likely to occur when companies have a lot of cash and plan takeovers as a short cut to expansion.

> *In a strong bull market, companies are cash-rich and merger-mad. This may signal a market peak is near.*

The vast size of corporate activity can have a big impact on the market. When the Glaxo bid actually went through, during April 1995, Glaxo paid Wellcome shareholders in cash. The institutions suddenly received a huge amount of free cash to reinvest. This money helped to boost the market at the time. Corporate activity with bids and mergers can make a big impression on your own portfolio, if one of the companies in which you have shares becomes the subject of a takeover. The share price can leap upwards, perhaps by 100p or more. This happened to many small investors holding the shares of the electricity distribution companies in 1995.

When takeover stories are widespread among lots of companies, it can indicate where we are in the economic cycle, as this urge to merge often occurs as the economic cycle is nearing maturity. It was notable in the early months of 1987, before the tremendous October crash. It can also happen after a deep recession, with the first stirrings of recovery. Companies with cash and ambitions to expand bid for other companies before the price of the shares in these target companies rises too much, making them more expensive to buy.

FINANCIAL ASSETS A-PLENTY

Another major influence on the shares we hold comes from the massive overall financial market which contains all the key financial assets that are freely traded on the world's markets. They include all forms of Government debt; short-term (**bills**) and medium- or long-term Government fixed-interest debt (**bonds**). In addition, there are **derivatives** of company shares (traded options) and futures options derived from the major market **indices**. These are directly linked to the corporate sector, because they 'derive' their value from the underlying shares or indices themselves. In addition there are assets in commodities such as base metals, oil and agricultural products, and precious metals which are all freely traded. There is a well-defined sequence for the way all these tradeable instruments fluctuate, and we will take a look at that sequence shortly.

It may feel safer to be part of the crowd,
but it might not help you to get rich.

THE BUSINESS CYCLE

A fourth major influence is the economic cycle itself. This generally takes between four to eight years to go through one complete turn and in the process it goes through a series of phases that is examined in more detail on pages 130–1 below. It is also known as the business cycle, a long-term phenomenon that includes all the fluctuations of booming economic activity followed by growth pauses, recessions or worse. These gyrations get reflected in the financial markets with a distinct time shift. The financial markets of interest rates, bonds, stocks and shares anticipate trends in the business cycle. *The markets are ahead of the news in the real economic world.*

POLITICAL STORMS

The last cycle to consider is politics, which is dominated by the parliamentary timetable. It is hard not to be cynical about the brazen manoeuvrings of politicians strutting around this cycle. Soon after an election, they adopt nasty belt-tightening plans, telling voters the economy is in a worse state than they had expected. This almost certainly means raising interest rates, which markets hate, because it increases the costs of servicing company loans. These extra expenses reduce their profits. Higher interest rates mean consumers also have less free money to spend after paying out higher interest charges on mortgages, credit card debts and other loans. If the public accounts are severely stretched, governments will raise tax rates, which hit companies and consumers in the same heavy-handed way.

The greatest mistake is to misread the data to make it fit with your initial expectations.

Later in the political cycle, when they are hoping to get re-elected, these same politicians, with a blatant flourish, may give voters back some of the cash they took from them two or three years earlier, perhaps by lowering interest rates or reducing income tax rates. At these times, the extra cash circulating in the economy will boost prices of bonds and shares. Markets are always happy when interest rates are falling and consumers are spending more money.

A CLUSTER OF CYCLES

All these cycles and influences are interacting in complicated ways, moving through an up-part of each cycle and on through a down-part. In general, all these interwoven movements are the cycles of activity that impact upon the markets and upon one another. Take the political cycle, for example. If the economy gets into a real mess, one might expect that no amount of juggling will help the election chances of an incompetent incumbent government. The electorate will ultimately take their revenge. But there are times when a government can be seriously blown off course by the turn events take which seem to be almost beyond its control. Britain's dramatic expulsion from the European Exchange Rate Mechanism on 16 September 1992 was an example of helpless officials and politicians bowled along by the sheer force of unforeseen factors operating against them.

On other occasions, the bond market can register its disapproval of government policies by refusing to buy the government debt (as **Gilt edged bonds**) that keeps the nation's accounting books balanced. This buyers' strike can be most serious. It may create such a crisis for politicians, they lose control of events. They may be driven along by the pressure of these circumstances, forced to do what the market wants, even if it is not what the politicians themselves would prefer to do. Investors and politicians alike should remember how powerful market forces can sometimes be.

Treat the market with respect, or it may suddenly bring you down to earth with a bump.

POINTERS TO WATCH

This brief sketch on how events affect the companies in your portfolio highlights what we want to know by tracking the market. There are several key pointers to what is happening to the real economy, outside the world of finance, which will help us to know what is going on. Broadly, they cover the following items:

i   *Will interest rates rise or fall?* Stock markets hate rising rates.
ii *When is the next general election?* As we have seen, political events can greatly influence the market.

iii *Are there serious economic problems in the pipeline* that the market is ignoring? Currency turbulence, rising inflation, balance of payments or large trade deficits can cause serious difficulties that cannot be ignored indefinitely.

iv *What stage in the economic cycle have other major markets reached,* e.g. Europe, USA and Japan? How will this affect our markets?

v   *At which stage of the economic cycle are we now in –* boom or bust? Is the economy growing or contracting?

MARKET MOVEMENTS

Market moves always precede events in the real economy. Both a rising market (a bull market) and a seriously falling market (a bear market) usually consist of three phases. Rising markets can extend over several years, for example, the long bull run from 1984 to 1987. During the first phase all the bad news about the current recession in the economy finally begins to be discounted. The jargon for this is that 'all the bad news is in the price'. The first hopes of recovery emerge. During the second phase these early hopes are confirmed and the real economy at last shows signs of improvement. The third, mature phase is one of great optimism and exaggerated expectations. This is the dangerous period, as a lot of hype and accordingly less real substance surrounds such exuberant optimism. In this period companies are flush with cash after years of grim belt-tightening during the recession. They are suddenly willing to pay absurdly high prices to buy companies in takeovers. The market is flush with enthusiasm and is only too happy to ignore any warning signs of trouble ahead. New issues rush to market to take advantage of the high prices. Many companies seek rights issues, to tap their shareholders for extra funds, while circumstances look rosy.

> *If bad news is expected and the news is good,*
> *the market will rejoice.*

The main bear or falling market is of a similar shape with three phases, this time in reverse. In the first phase, the good news is built into share prices and the first signs of recession in the real economy emerge. The stock market anticipates the peak in the real economy, declining before the actual recession begins.

During the second phase prices fall back over one month or several months, often by between 15 to 30 per cent of the preceding upturn. The recession itself is now clearly visible in many areas of activity and the sense of pessimism spreads. The third or final down phase is often one of maximum gloom and despondency. There may be a sudden huge sell-off as investors, who were desperately hanging on for recovery, finally lose their nerve. If this occurs in heavy volume, it can signal an imminent turning point. After a massive selling climax, fewer panicky sellers are left, so the market upturn can begin.

Selling after a big fall is incredibly stupid. But it's a luxury everyone seems to indulge in every now and then.

MARKING TIME

One interesting feature to note is that although serious bear markets usually have pauses when bargain hunters appear, they are often short and sharp. This may be because on the slide down there are generally fewer people who are willing to come in and buy. During the upturn, each drop in prices is used by investors to re-enter the market, which explains why the rise proceeds in a jagged three spurts up and two spurts down.

In 1990, the peak for economic output was reached in March and the market had already begun falling in January, although it recovered by the early summer. When Saddam Hussein invaded Kuwait on 2 August, the market took fright. It fell heavily for about two months to hit a low at the end of September. And the next bull market really took off the day the Gulf War began, on 16 January 1991, when the markets realized the United Nations forces would defeat Saddam.

In 1994, when the UK market peaked on 2 February, the fall was dramatic: over 600 points was chopped off the FT-SE 100 index in the next five months. After another nine months of up–down trading, the next bull market surge began in March

1995 and was still broadly intact seventeen months later, at the end of August 1996. In October 1995, manufacturing output finally got back to the level it had reached at the March 1990 peak.

THE MARKET'S SHIFTING PHASES

When we look at the way in which the shifting phases of the market unfold, we have to remember that in the financial markets everything is relative. All the influencing factors interact one with another in an infinitely complex way. As one factor changes, many others will be forced to change. So events in any one of the interlocking cycles may have repercussions in any of the others or in the overall picture. Traditionally, however, the markets fluctuate through a well-defined sequence. This is shown in figure 21.

i   The first market to hit a peak or a bottom is the *short-term fixed interest government debt market, termed Bills.* It is the earliest indicator that investors have had a change of mood. The level of 90-day deposit rates and money market rates, recorded daily in the financial press, give a clue as to what is happening, because these rates move in the opposite direction from the price of the short bonds. On this see-saw, as the price of a bond rises, the level of the interest rate falls. The markets love falling interest rates, as they herald a spending boom, which is good for company profits.

ii *The longer dated bonds begin to rise* shortly after the short dated Bills start rising. They tend to react slightly later. A fall in the bond price (with a rise in the **yield** or interest paid on it) means investors are worrying about rising inflation. Conversely, if bonds begin rising, investors believe inflation will stay low and the capital gains they make on their rising bonds will compensate for the fall in the yield or interest earned.

iii *The stock market* is the third phase in the sequence to show a pronounced move. It often peaks when it has absorbed the prospect of all the good news. This moment arrives before

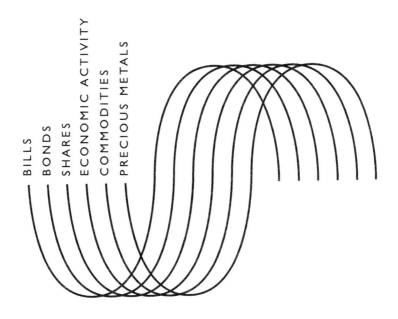

Figure 21 Diagram of sequence of fluctuations in financial markets with an actual example showing UK company earnings/share cycle 1991–6. (Adapted from charts by Lars Tveda and James Capel.)

the economy itself peaks, because the markets are ahead of the news, both good and bad. The stock market is a leading indicator for the economic cycle. As interest rates start rising, buying shares on credit is more expensive, so there are fewer buyers.

Genius is a short memory in a bull market.   J.K. Galbraith

iv   *Economic activity goes on expanding* after the stock market begins to fall. It can take three to six months to hit a peak after the stock market has begun its decline.

v   *Commodities*, such as base metals (copper, tin, zinc, etc.) and soft commodities, like sugar, wheat, cotton, etc., peak after economic activity has peaked. This is because a sudden increase in capital investment by companies may occur during the last phases of the economic upturn, leading to bottle-necks. This creates a rise in commodity usage, and their prices surge in tandem.

vi   *Precious metals: gold, silver and platinum* are the last assets in the sequence to show a rise. This occurs at a time when shares and long bonds have both begun to fall, and inflation is rising. Precious metals are then seen as a safe haven, although in recent years, with an explosion of interest in derivative markets such as traded options and futures contracts, the role of precious metals in this shifting phase sequence has been reduced.

WHERE IS THE MARKET HEADING?

Finally, we turn to the main phases of the cycle in economic activity. As a do-it-myself investor, the big question I ask myself is, 'Where is the market going?' Often, the vital buying or selling questions ultimately depend on where in the bull/bear cycle we are. Judging market direction depends on where we are in the business cycle. It was fashionable, in the heady 1980s, to say the business cycle had been eliminated, but during the early 1990s, having suffered one of the longest, toughest recessions since the 1930s, this rosy view has been forgotten.

If the story for your company is brilliant, forget the market's mood and stay with your share.

If we look at the state of the economy when the stock market begins to rise, a patchy recovery is emerging, but signs of slump are everywhere. Inflation will be low, as there is less activity and low demand. Without the rising demand for goods, inflation will stay low. At the bottom of the most recent severe recession, 1990–2 inflation fell towards a 25-year low and the unemployment total almost reached 3 million. The media focused on the miserable recession and its endless stream of bad news, but canny investors will have noticed that fixed interest bond and share prices were beginning to creep up.

As the stock market is a forward indicator, share prices can rise for six to nine months before the economic upturn actually arrives. The market boom anticipates the mature stage of the economic expansion but it will peak before any overheating occurs in the real economy. This over-expansion hampers further growth. Adverts extolling the splendid performance of unit and investment trusts fill the press; the figures for new money put into these collective funds begin to rise and may hit all-time records. Small private investors have read all the media hype and are piling into the main collective funds in droves.

The point in the cycle when bull markets end is, all too often, when investors realize that interest rates have reached a low and are set to rise. Sadly, in the past, the most reliable indicator that the market is nearing its peak has been statistics showing private investors are plunging back into unit and investment trusts. The sales will reach all-time highs.

The next market crash will only come when you are fully invested.

In a modern industrial economy the business cycle has become closely linked with the price and availability of **credit**; crudely, this means the level of interest rates which either encourage more borrowing or ration money for loans. Consequently, the onset of rising interest rates completes the business cycle by ushering in the next decline as fear of another credit squeeze grows.

THE STAGES OF THE ECONOMIC CYCLE

The economic cycle is like a compass with the needle moving all the time, through various points. Knowing the four main phases of every cycle helps us to fix where we are now. By working out where we actually are in the cycle, we can assess the most likely future trend for the market. To do this we look at key pointers, like levels of interest rates, inflation, unemployment and economic activity (measured by the **Gross Domestic Product** – figures which state the amount of goods and services officially recorded as produced in one calendar year). This essential background information is helpful for investment decisions. In detail, therefore, the four main phases of every cycle are as follows: slump, expansion, boom and decline.

The shares you buy hoping they will rise sky high, might suddenly collapse.

i *Slump*. The economy is flat with reduced spending all round. Interest rates fall to persuade industry to invest and people to borrow more. Unemployment is rising, companies go bankrupt, investment is low, the property market is depressed. Companies have low earnings and banks have bad debts. Media and politicians brood on the bad news but bonds begin to rise as interest rates fall. The best profits from shares are usually made in the first two years of the bull market as the economy expands out of recession.

ii *Economic expansion* begins with a slow upward creep. It gathers pace as interest rates reach a trough and companies start reporting rising order books. Recovery is patchy and intermittent. There can be false dawns. The media turn from pessimism to optimism halfway through the upturn.

iii   *Boom*. The economy is booming. Bottlenecks and shortages in labour, goods, services and commodities appear. Both interest rates and inflation start rising; the economy over-heats. Unemployment peaks or begins to fall. The stock market booms; merger and takeover activity increases; new issues flood onto the market; sales of unit and investment trusts reach record levels. Companies and consumers take on more debt. The media is very positive. Everyone is optimistic. Share prices start to fall before the economy peaks as investors have anticipated the boom. The market is ahead of the economy.

The next thing you know, the market is falling, taking your shares down in the general slide. Before you have time to think, you are sitting on a loss.

iv   *Decline*. This is the inevitable result of the boom because the economy invariably overshoots. The decline is a way of wiping out excessive debt. Private consumption drops off. Industry has rising excess capacity. Inflation rises to a peak in the middle of the decline; many interest-rate-sensitive companies face bankruptcy, as do those who over-expanded during the boom. The media turn pessimistic. Share prices are falling but bond prices rise, anticipating falling inflation. And here we go again . . . back to the slump.

DISRUPTIONS INTRUDE

A classic cycle like this seldom happens. There will rarely be a pure sequence, because unforeseen shocks often intrude to affect the flow of the phases. Although these outline stages always occur, events are rarely so clear cut because of these disruptive outside factors. In recent years the build-up to the Gulf War in the autumn of 1990 and the turbulence of currencies at the time of the Exchange Rate Mechanism crisis of 1992 are examples of how difficult outside influences can adversely affect the markets.

During the six months before the January 1991 Gulf War began, this major international event was seriously unsettling the markets. Severely affected market sectors were travel, entertainments, tourism, and hotel industries. The value of shares in these sectors fell sharply.

Other major factors may play a part in disrupting the smooth sequence, such as the political agenda for electing a new party leader or a general election timetable. Then there is the abrupt drama of a crash, as occurred in October 1987. Share prices collapsed suddenly, instead of falling more steadily. The economy was buffeted by large, abnormal shock waves. The central banks intervened to steady the markets after this massive loss of confidence. They lowered interest rates to ensure there was no crippling credit squeeze in the aftermath of the crisis. Markets do not act so well as financial barometers when such major destabilizing price movements occur.

THE CYCLE OF SECTORS

As the business cycle unfolds in stages, so the cycle from bull to bear market progresses with some sectors leading while others lag. Early in the upturn, the biggest risers are consumer-related sectors, as this is where the first recovery occurs in the real economy. Food retailers, utilities, consumer goods, pharmaceuticals, stores, banks, finance and insurance lead the pack. With more expansion, industrial shares are again sought, including building materials, contractors, construction, general engineering, textiles and consumer durables, such as motors. These sectors often peak alongside the main indices. The final, third phase consists of typical laggards, shares related to capital investment and commodities. They include chemicals, machine-tools, metal-working, mines, transport and aviation.

Knowing what information you are looking for is not the same as being able to lay your hands on it.

CHECK LIST OF MARKET MOVERS

You can monitor some of the main activities which move share prices. They include all the major unexpected national or international events. Key people, in major countries, such as the USA, UK, Germany, Japan, etc., including politicians and central bankers, can also move prices, by making important speeches, being elected or dying suddenly in office. Popular analysts, such as Nick Knight, Barton Biggs, or famous investors like George Soros or Jim Slater, can all move prices if they do or say something that has an important bearing on certain shares or markets. Shares mentioned in the newspapers or the popular newsletters as tips often move prices, but they might fall back again after a few days if there is insufficient follow-through support.

Major political events make a big impact on markets, as we saw with the 1992 General Election, discussed in Chapter 4. Other political events can seriously affect the markets. Recent bouts of Tory disunity had an adverse impact, as did some politically motivated interest rate changes, which the market disliked. Major political events in other countries can have similar effects, if they are serious enough to have global consequences.

The most important market-moving financial events will happen when you are on holiday – abroad.

The level of interest rates is another key indicator to watch, as we have already seen how it changes during the stages of the economic cycle. Interest rate changes can alert us to a major market turning point, whenever they reach a peak or a trough.

Famous entrepreneurs sometimes take a large holding in a **shell company** and this can move the price higher. In 1993, George Soros entered into a partnership with the property company British Land. The share price rose about 50p on the news. Entrepreneurs often buy into shell companies; examples include Nigel Wray when he took a large stake in Carlisle in the spring of 1994, and together with Ian Gowrie-Smith formerly of Medeva, in February 1995, both took large stakes in a small company called Black & Edgington, aiming to convert it into a pharmaceuticals group, later renamed Skypharma.

COMPANY NEWS THAT MOVES SHARE PRICES

Several company events can move the share price, depending on whether the news is good, bad, or unexpected. If a company announces excellent, or conversely terrible interim or final results, the price jumps to reflect the figures. Major unexpected news items produce a similar effect. These include bids, takeovers, rights issues, major contracts, directors dealings, management changes, boardroom coups, new products, new management, decisions to float subsidiaries, or to obtain a listing on a foreign exchange, such as New York or Tokyo, sudden profits warnings and optimistic trading statements, chairmans' reports at the annual general meeting on current trading conditions. When companies are floated on the markets as new issues, offers for sale and placings, stake building by institutional shareholders in early dealings can all push prices higher very smartly.

TRACK THE NEWS EVENTS

Traders, institutional investors, speculators and small investors often take a lively interest in the key economic statistics that affect the performance of the economy, either nationally or globally. They include another raft of facts and figures, which give clues on how well or badly the economy is doing. The most notable are: figures for inflation (the RPI, retail prices index), the level of the Government's debt (the PSBR, the public sector borrowing requirement), retail sales, balance of payments with export and import statistics, CBI reports which give an indication of how companies view their trading prospects and unemployment figures. Similar data for other countries, including Germany, America, Japan, can have an effect on the UK market, especially if there is an unexpected figure, either good or bad.

MARKET PEAKS

The coincidence of high unemployment and the stock market peaking together suggests investors are insensitive to the misfortune of others, but there is a logical explanation for this apparent cynicism. Rising unemployment means productivity is rising. More output per head enhances company profitability, which is what the stock market celebrates. We will look at signals that alert us to market peaks and troughs in Chapter 8, when we discuss ways to monitor your portfolio.

> *You can sometimes tell when a peak is due because influential people start spouting silly sayings.*

Each business cycle differs in length and special factors, so how can we use this general information to decide where the stock market is heading? For the 1990–2 recession, figures for Gross Domestic Product (GDP) showed 10 quarters of decline – the longest fall in GDP since records began. Officially the economy began its decline in mid-1990 and fell for thirty consecutive months. Stock market volatility in 1990, 1991 and 1992 reflected false dawns for a recovery that failed to materialize. Norman Lamont's 'green shoots' of recovery proved persistently difficult to spot.

Interest rate falls accelerated after Britain left the Exchange Rate Mechanism in September 1992, and that event proved to be the major turning point for the next big bull market. It signalled a break away from holding interest rates at punishingly high levels to keep within the fixed exchange rate band Britain had decided upon when entering the mechanism two years earlier. This level was far too high, as the real economy fell into one of the most savage recessions for decades. As it was later learned that the British authorities decided upon this level without consulting any European authorities, this may explain why the Europeans did not rally to help the British during the September 1992 crisis. As in every financial situation, poor decisions often come back to haunt their originators.

As Britain left the Exchange Rate Mechanism, the first hesitant signs of rising consumer demand from car, property and retail sales figures were emerging. I was not fully conversant with the market cycle then, or the role lower interest rates would play in boosting the prices of shares. However, I realized from financial reports that most commentators welcomed Britain's expulsion from the Exchange Rate Mechanism. At such times, it is clearly profitable to follow the crowd, even if you cannot work out the details of why they are celebrating. This event was a significant turning point. The stock market rose from a FT-SE 100 low of 2,280 in August 1992 to hit an all-time high of 3,918 on 28 August 1996, a 71.8 per cent rise in four years.

Following the moods of the market will help you avoid buying at the peak and selling at the bottom.

IS THIS THE PEAK?

Testing periodically for a market peak helps to focus on the four phases of the economic cycle. Various key factors affect the current market's mood, and therefore share prices. The future direction of interest rates is far more important than the actual level they reach. Occasionally it makes sense to run through the factors that influence share prices for good or ill. Take the case of spring 1996. Most commentators expected the market to show lacklustre performance for the year, as it was still near an April all-time FT-SE 100 high of 3,857. Interest rates were expected to fall further, as growth had slowed. If the stock market peaks when interest rates are threatening to rise, this may not occur until later in 1996. Interest rates may also fall in Germany and France, which would be a plus sign for UK rates to fall as well. However, David Schwartz, who edits the *Schwartz Stock Market Handbook*, cautions that stock market history shows the next downturn is already overdue. Prices have risen every quarter since June 1994. If they stayed up by end-March 1996 (as they did), the stock market would have seen seven rising consecutive quarters, a rare occurrence historically.

Over the next few months during the latter half of 1996 and early 1997, the political cycle will become increasingly important. Markets traditionally do not like big-spending Labour governments; in the past, they raised more government debt and accepted high levels of inflation. In 1996, the Tory Government will worry increasingly about its political revival; it may reduce tax or interest rates, to create a mini-boom which boosts bond and share prices. This could backfire if investors scorn cynical political giveaways. On balance, however, as the market may prefer to see the Tories re-elected, it may allow more monetary slackness than is appropriate.

This is the type of reasoning I apply when I am trying to gauge where we are now and what might happen in the short term.

One useful signal to watch for is more small investor participation; there should be rising sales of unit and investment trusts and new issues of funds with expensive publicity, to tempt private investors to buy. When they are enthusiastic buyers, the institutions have fully discounted the good news and are looking ahead to the next economic decline and another round of 'pass-the-parcel'.

When the small investor is fully invested, share prices have nowhere to go but down.

'All you need to know is what the market has actually done, not what it might do,' says William O'Neil, in *How to Make Money in Stocks*. This profound comment reminds the investor who is prepared to do some careful homework that he need not speculate endlessly on what the market might do next, which is totally unproductive, if he is willing to note closely what the market is actually doing now. Once you know how the market, financial assets and the real economy move through their different phases, you can let the market tell its own story.

When you send a fool to market, the merchants rejoice.

CHAPTER 7

The action plan

Initially, it does no harm to fall in love with your shares, but this could be costly if you grow too attached to them when the time comes that they should be sold.

When you have considered both the outline and detailed part of your system, and have started to run a small test paper portfolio, you can plan your investment actions and then set about acting on the plan. In this chapter we look at your action plan, with set routines to stay in touch with events. How you monitor the market and the shares you are either watching or actually holding is covered in Chapter 8.

Experienced investors with long-term goals for their portfolios (spanning five to ten years) might lock their shares safely away and not look at then again for one or more years. This is not a policy I would recommend for do-it-yourself investors. No matter how carefully you have selected the shares in your portfolio, the chances are that perhaps four in every ten will not perform as you expected. It makes sense carefully to monitor new investments for at least six months, just to satisfy yourself that they are performing well. If you want to build a sizeable nest egg, the object of your patient planning is not to choose a superbly well-balanced portfolio, but to find a group of small, aggressively growing companies to produce large gains. After holding your shares for about six months, you will be better able to judge whether or not they can be left for the long term.

If you want to become a seriously rich investor, first you must learn how to survive in the stock market.

YOUR DAILY/WEEKLY WORKOUT

If you have decided to use the minimum of expensive additional equipment until you have gained some hands-on experience, you should set up a few basic files to keep your records tidy. At the very least, you will need an up-to-date account of your share transactions, for buying and selling, with details of your capital gains or losses, cash balances, interest paid on the cash and dividends due, with the amounts to be received and the dates when they will be paid. This can be done for the paper portfolio, to get you working correctly.

It sounds like too much file-keeping, but it can be a simple exercise. I keep all the main details of my current portfolio on the back of an old compliment slip. A second slip records details of each deal. I note the date, the time, the name of the broker who did the trade (in case of disagreements), the number of shares bought or sold, the price dealt and the transaction costs, so I can check the main details when the contract note arrives. Details are shown in the examples on page 141.

A third compliment slip records running cash balance totals for the joint portfolio and our three PEPs (two General PEPs and one Single Company PEP) so I always know the amount of free cash available. I now have a simple computer program to enter all these details once a week. But on a daily basis, I still prefer entering everything on my simple manual system, as I have done for the past six years. All the used compliment slips are clipped together, in a tidy bundle. As one slip is filled, a new one is started. The old ones are filed, in case I want to check back later.

No records for PEPs are necessary, but I keep them for easy checking on my deals, especially when contract notes arrive. To value the portfolio, I separate PEPs from the main portfolio with two columns for the shares held in our four portfolios. One column lists the main portfolio, which is shrinking as the PEP portfolios grow with each new year's additions; the other column lists shares held in the two General PEPs, and one Single Company PEP.

Dividing my savings into blocks has worked out in practice exactly as I thought it might when I set out my initial plans in 1990. The cash in the main portfolio took a big hit in 1994, due to many months of falling markets and rebuilding work in the house, but I made good gains in the summer of 1995 to rebuild the fund. Recouping money from profitable investments to pay for emergency outlays is precisely what successful investment is all about for people like me, who are mainly searching for financial security from their savings. I have gained enormous extra confidence to face whatever nasty financial shocks may be thrown at me in future. I see this gain in confidence as one of my greatest profits from learning how to be a do-it-myself investor.

There is no better confidence-builder than watching your invested money grow.

A DIARY IS A USEFUL AID

If you keep a single book or a page-a-day diary, with the key 'bullet point' notes you have made during your reading, plus the details of your paper portfolio, you might try keeping a proper diary of your thoughts and investment ideas, to help check on your progress. This is a useful learning aid for novice investors. It records your immediate thoughts and acts, to which you can refer later, when you are analysing your successes or failures. It gives a

---

CURRENT PORTFOLIO

	PEPS					Joint account			
Date B'ght	Share	No.	Price (p)	Cost (£)	Date B'ght	Share	No.	Price (p)	Cost (£)
					15/2/95	FCK	1850	215	4047.5
1/5/95	TSP	1400	452	6419.5					
27/6/95	CDA	3800	118	4556.5					
29/6/95	UNP	1429	203	2966.0					
7/8/95	CRO	2000	183	3728.5					
9/8/95	MA	1000	103	1060.5	9/8/95	MA	3000	102	3110.5

Total No. of shares 6

Dividend details

Share	X-D Date	Amt (p)	Total Due £	Act No.	Paid on	
FCK	14/8/95	0.75p	13.87	XXYYZZ	2.10	pd
TSP	11/9/95	1.00p	14.00	AABBCC	19.10	pd

Share Codes	Share Names
TSP	Telspec
CDA	Coda
UNP	Unipalm
CRO	Chiruscience
MA	Maid
FCK	Filtronic Comtek

record of how you planned each investment. This again will be helpful at a later stage for judging how good your forecasts or target prices were.

> *You are in better control of events when you become more aware of what makes the market move.*

The diary keeps all the important information and records together, in one tidy place. This is perhaps the best reason for keeping a diary, so you never accidentally throw away scraps of paper on which you scribbled information for referring back to later. I only began to keep a real investment diary in January 1995. I find it is an invaluable investment aid. Having a reliable record of past experiences to refer back to is a big boon for all investors.

AN EXAMPLE OF HOW TO KEEP RECORDS

Dealings records

15/2/95   Joint Act No. XXYYZZ   Frank   8.15 a.m.
Bought 1850 Filtronic Comtek at 215p

          Settles on 1/3/95 1850 x £2.15   =   £3977.50
                                          + £50.00 commission
                                          + £20.00 stamp duty*
                       Total cost   =   £4047.50

          average cost/share 218.8p

          * stamp duty: (3977.50 x .005 =£19.89) rounded up = £20.00

27/6/95   My General Pep No. AABBCC Jonathon   9.25 a.m.
Bought 3800 Coda at 1.18p

          Settles on 7/7/95 3800 x £1.18   =   £4484.00
                                          + £50.00 commission
                                        + £22.50 stamp duty*
                       Total cost   =   £4556.50

          average cost/share 120p

          * stamp duty: (4484 x .005 = £22.42) rounded up =£22.50

GET ORGANIZED

Once you set up a methodical plan of action, it will work smoothly and take less time to operate successfully. A necessary starting point for me was to keep simple records of significant stock market data, so I would develop a better 'feel' about market events. You become more informed as you track the data on a regular basis.

TO TURN OR NOT TO TURN?

By doing this regularly, you will also learn how to recognize days when the data is quite exceptional, either in one or in many respects. Exceptional figures often indicate a turning point. These are the crucial times when either the confident optimists or gloomy pessimists are about to influence the direction of the market. This might be decided by 'the sheer weight of numbers'. The turning point is on hand, to be followed, if the same mood persists, by the establishment of a new trend. This is why the figures on stock market activity are so useful. They give vital clues on how this event is shaping up.

These periods often mark the crucial days or weeks when a strong bull market begins to boil over and run out of steam, or a prolonged bear phase fizzles out and a new up-trend could begin to take hold. Judging when these turns occur as near as possible to the turn itself is one of the most important ways of increasing your profits, so that you can have more cash invested soon after the next upturn arrives. You also want to know how to protect your profits and hold on to them, soon after the next big downturn begins.

Investing ahead of the turn is a high-risk strategy.

Anticipating a major turning point is often reasonably easy, but, actually timing its arrival is almost impossible, because so many diverse factors are operating to influence the final outcome. Moreover, at a major turning point the bulls or bears will both be energetic and visible. At a peak, the bulls are hoping new highs are imminent, but if they are not, the pessimists will gain the upper hand. At a trough, the bears think bad news will worsen, sending the market even lower, but then the optimists return and the market recovers. Guessing which group will win these turning-point skirmishes is more akin to gambling than investing, and can result in losses.

At these turns, the market sometimes swings about with big moves up or down, often of 30, 40 or even 50 points, in one direction, followed by an equally wild swing next day in the other direction. For this reason, investing ahead of the turn is highly risky. Before the turn actually arrives, it is impossible to be sure that it will happen. Contrary to your expectations, the previous trend may find enough support to reassert itself and continue as before, so the expected turning point will abort. Alternatively, the bull/bear struggle may not get cleanly resolved one way or the other, and the market moves in a drifting trading range until one side can finally swing the result decisively in its favour.

To ensure you do not act in haste, you can look for clusters of data that indicate the turn has arrived, plus confirmatory signals from the charts. The data clusters are the technical indicators we mentioned in Chapter 2. If you can judge the turn close to when it actually happens, you can buy early for the rise or sell early for the fall; together, buying early and selling early are two of the greatest ways of making big profits. This was one of Nathan Rothschild's favourite recipes for investment success.

I never buy at the bottom and I always sell too soon.
Nathan Rothschild

INDICATORS FOR THE TURNS

Everyone develops their own set of preferred indicators to help assess where the market is now. I like to keep a wide range of daily figures, to give me a broad view of many technical features operating in the market. I have kept a series of 15 indicators since January 1993. Most of them have proved especially useful, but some have been dropped and replaced by others as my interests change. Once several pages have been ruled up to record these daily figures, I spend only a few minutes a day finding them on the Summary screen of my *Market Eye*, and in the *Financial Times* on the following morning. I enter these figures in columns on my daily record. Most of them appear on the back two pages of the 'Companies and Markets' section of the *Financial Times* (three back pages on Saturdays). Busy investors could keep all the papers and enter the figures they want to monitor once a week only.

You should not become a slave to your records. They are only aids to alert you to major market movements.

DAILY TRACKING

I follow very few international figures, tracking them only to keep alert for key events that may affect the UK market, as this is where my money is invested. I record the American Dow Jones Industrial Average index (DJIA), together with the actual number of points change from the previous day and the total number of shares traded on the New York Stock Exchange. Events in America often move other world markets, so it is important to know what happens there.

I watch the broadly based S&P index when I expect big moves in America, but at other times I ignore it. I also follow the technology-rich Nasdaq Composite index because I hold a mini-technology portfolio. I worry that if the Nasdaq index took a sudden plunge, it might affect my UK share portfolio. I also record the Tokyo Nikkei Dow index with its daily change. I keep the US and Nikkei Dow data to judge international moods as markets today are globally interconnected.

I invest only in shares listed on the UK stock market. I do not want to spend too much time on tracking and I try not to get diverted into time-wasting detours where I lose focus. So I concentrate on a narrow group of several UK indicators. These include the closing daily FT-SE 100 index, plus the actual change in number of points (not percentages) from the previous day; the closing **FT-SE Mid 250 index** and the closing **FT-SE 350 index**, both with the change in points from the previous day. I record the **FT-SE SmallCap index** (using the one which excludes investment trusts, as I have no investment trust shares), because I want to see how the index for the very small shares is performing relative to the other indices.

Finally, I record the closing level for the FT-SE-A All-Share index covering about 910 shares together with its percentage change from the previous day's close. The last entry with this crop of figures is a record of the dividend yield on the FT-SE-A All-Share index, as a way of gauging if prices are rising too high. The best time to purchase shares is thought to be when this yield is around 4 or over. As it falls below about 3.95, shares are considered to be getting expensive.

Don't waste energy fretting about things you cannot change.
Concentrate on the things you can change.

DECIPHER THE MOVES

Useful clues on the performance of the market arise from this welter of data when some of the indices are rising and others are falling. This is an ambiguous signal and therefore not a convincing sign to act on, as it indicates a lopsided market movement when only part of the market is moving ahead. I feel wary when some indices are rising while others fall, even when I think I know why they are diverging. *The best signals occur when all the indices are rising strongly, or falling heavily, together.* This can be a significant pointer. It is an even stronger signal if the moves, measured in number of points, are fairly large, right across the board. For example, a rise of over 20 points on several of these indices could be significant.

Sometimes there are clear reasons for a diverging index. For instance, the utility companies – water, gas, electricity – are listed on the FT-SE Mid 250 index. If there is a bid story for one of them, the whole sector forges ahead. Conversely, when there are scare stories about increased regulation for utilities, or a windfall tax, they all fall in unison, again affecting the FT-SE Mid 250 index only.

When all the indices make a strong rise in unison, and a bullish signal emerges, records of the day's volumes of shares traded may give a confirmation that the bullish trend is developing well. A vigorously rising trend offers the best type of market for making superb profits, so you want to know how strong the up-trend is likely to be. To test this on a daily basis, I keep records of each day's total volume of shares traded up to 5.00 p.m. (in millions), together with the number of actual trades that were done (in thousands). As small investors do not trade after the market closes, I do not bother with the 6.00 p.m. figures. However, between 5.00 and 6.00 p.m., these figures would give a good indication of what the major institutional investors alone were doing. I have never recorded this figure, but it could be a useful indicator to show whether the fund managers are investing in strength.

On dividing the total number of shares traded by the number of trades done, I obtain the average size of each trade. This gives me an idea of how large the average trade was. If the average size is only about 17,000 to 19,000 shares per trade, it indicates a lot of small transactions, perhaps by private investors. However, when the number of shares per average trade is high, say above 25,000, it suggests plenty of institutional activity. At a market peak, there can be a massive turnover figure but only a tiny movement in the indices. This is another good indication that the struggle between the bulls and bears is unresolved. Despite lots of transactions, neither was able to shift the indices decisively to their advantage. This can indicate the bulls are losing momentum, while at the trough it might mean the bears are running out of steam.

If a massive block of shares changes hands between two institutions, the huge volume is due to double-counting. This is a one-off item, although it happens quite frequently, but I ignore it. Keeping precise stock market records is not my aim. I simply want to watch the big picture unfold, to help my investment decision-taking.

If the market has risen strongly, it is a fair assumption that most of the trades will be on the buying side, and vice versa if the market has fallen heavily. These figures give useful clues as to what may be going on. On an 'up' day, very heavy volume, with large institutional activity (visible through the average size of each trade), indicates strong buying by the fund managers. This is a very positive, bullish indicator. It is even better if all the FT-SE indices I am tracking are rising together with large daily movements. This is strong confirmation of a rising market.

As we saw in Chapter 4, the charts may also be confirming the emergence of this new trend. There will be golden crosses, moving averages marching up in line under the index, new highs for the index, new breakouts or gaps. Any or all of these indicators may now appear.

It is wonderful news if you have most of your money invested in the market just as it begins a strong rise.

If there is a sharp setback in the market on fairly low volume, it suggests the fund managers are not selling. If they are still invested, it could be wise to wait, as the bullish mood might return. The low volume may indicate the market-makers are slashing prices, to ward off a lot of selling. In these situations, if you think the up-trend will soon recommence, you could even add to your favourite share positions, once again putting you ahead of the institutional crowd. To reduce the risks of being wrong, choose a share where the fundamentals make you feel very positive about buying a holding and the chart has just broken out of a congestion area, as discussed in Chapter 4.

TECHNICAL INDICATORS

Other figures I record every day include the numbers of shares making new highs, the numbers making new lows and the difference between the two. I then add (or deduct) that difference to (or from) the cumulative daily total, which goes all the way back to when my records began, in January 1993. I try to eliminate foreign shares, if they are quickly obvious, like foreign banks, and UK-listed American and Canadian shares. This is because I want to focus on the broad activity for UK quoted companies. If the odd one or two get through my net, it is not critical. The broad sweep of events is what I am trying to track.

You can often judge the strength of a rising or falling market from these figures. During a strong bull market the number of shares making new highs on a daily basis can be well over 200, while during a dreary downturn, the number of new lows is correspondingly high.

The market is only a phone call away.

WHEN TRACKING EARNS ITS KEEP

The period from December 1993 to March 1994, when a big market peak arrived and then passed, gives a good indication of how you can get to know what is going on by taking the trouble to do this simple daily 10-minute tracking task. During December 1993 the markets all around the world were roaring ahead, almost in unison. The numbers of shares hitting new highs rose above 300 on five days; there were two days with over 400 new highs and on 29 December, the figure was an astonishing 512. This was on a day when most people would not be bothering with the market and the volumes were faily low. My portfolio was growing by leaps and bounds.

HAS THE PEAK ARRIVED?

The dramatic contrast between these massive new daily high figures, which continued right through January 1994 and after early February, is instructive for revealing how to identify an important market turning point. I learned a great deal by analysing these figures in detail as I wrote this chapter. In retrospect, I can see that I made the right selling decisions in February 1994 but I re-entered the market too soon, later in the year before the downturn was nearing its end.

On 4 February, the new highs and lows were still showing a bullish tack. There were 292 new highs and only 11 new lows. But on Monday, 7 February, there were only 84 new highs and 21 new lows. This was indicating a change of mood, but other figures in my records showed just how big this mood swing might prove to be.

The evidence becomes clearer when we look at the story of the other share movements I record. These involve the numbers of shares that advanced (rose) and the numbers that declined (fell) each day, plus the difference between the two and again, I take the cumulative daily running total, recorded since January 1993. Finally, I note the numbers of shares that stayed unchanged every day. From the advancing, declining and unchanged totals given on the back pages of the *Financial Times*, I always deduct the figures for advancing, declining or unchanged for the gilts or fixed interest stocks, as I try to concentrate on UK equities alone. These figures can also be highly illuminating on the state of the market. They become even more useful once you have several months, or years of data, so that you can refer back to see what happened on similar occasions in the past.

CONFIRMATORY FIGURES

For example, on 7 February 1994, the day the stock market turned decisively down, and the number of new highs fell dramatically, there were only 179 advances and *a colossal 1993 declining shares*. This was the largest number of declining shares I had ever recorded. It was such a large number I entered it in red, so I could easily spot it in the welter of black ballpoint entries. On that momentous day, an incredibly low figure of 447 shares were unchanged. The normal range of unchanged shares is between 1,550 and 1,750. Although on its own, I could not tell if these figures reflected genuine trades or were simply market-makers protecting their positions, the sum total of indicators I follow was pointing decisively to a market top.

The volume of shares traded on that eventful day was also unique. The number of shares traded by 5.00 p.m. was heavy at 894.3 million and the number of trades was *an astonishing 54,033,* again the largest number of trades per day I have ever noted. The average trade size was low, at 16,551. This relatively low figure for the average trade size suggests many small investors may have been selling.

The FT-SE 100 index (see Figure 22) gave a confirmation that trouble was brewing; it fell by a massive 56.3 points on the day. And this must have been in response to a turbulently falling Wall Street on the previous Friday, where the Dow Jones Industrial Average recorded a massive drop of 96.24 on 4 February. Now that I know how the story unfolded during February 1994, I would immediately take avoiding action if I saw a similar combination of signals. They were really screaming 'Sell!' The stock market fell for six months from early February. If I had simply reduced my portfolio and not reinvested until much later in the year, my money would have been far better protected than it actually was.

There are a few occasions when the evidence for action is
so strong, all the confirmatory signals start
screaming at you.

In this example, we clearly see, even without consulting the FT-SE indices charts, that all the key technical indicators I keep records of were confirming 7 February as a significant turning-point. The abrupt change in the new highs and lows, the tiny number of advances against a massive number of declines, the noteworthy three-volume figures, especially the enormous number of actual trades, and the huge drop in the FT-SE 100 and the US Dow Jones Industrial Average indices, all indicated a downturn was imminent.

In addition, there was one key piece of fundamental news that sent shock waves around the global markets. The Federal Reserve Board of America, the central bank, had raised interest rates by 0.25 per cent. Although this was a minute rise, it signalled a change in the Board's attitude to rates, as it was the very first rise in interest rates for five years. Collectively, this tiny reverse move was so unexpected, all the world's share and bond markets simultaneously took fright.

And the FT-SE 100 chart was giving me the same cautionary message – INVESTORS BEWARE. The line of the index itself stood 460 points above the level of the long-term, 200-day moving average, an unprecedentedly large gap. The index had risen strongly since September 1993 and almost vertically throughout December. At some stage, the 200-day moving average would have to make contact again with the index. The fall was rapid, once it began, for the index swiftly cut down through the 20- and 50-day moving averages, within a few days of the February peak, making two dead crosses on the chart. It continued plunging, to shoot down through the still-rising 200-day average by late March, to create a third dead cross. The steep decline did not end until late June and after several months of an up–down trading range, the new upturn did not seriously begin until March 1995 as seen in figures 5 and 8.

At that time, the 200-day moving average at last stopped falling. By mid-March it was, in fact, just turning up and beginning to rise slightly. This proved to be a very bullish indicator because it coincided with a golden cross as the index rose through both the 20- and 50-day averages. By late March, the 20-day average rose through the 200-day average to make a golden cross, followed in early April by a golden cross as the 50-day average rose through the rising 200-day average. By mid-April, all three moving averages were rising one behind the other, and in line below the rising index. The bullish signals were all nicely in place to indicate this was a good time to re-enter the market. It looks so easy in hindsight.

Investing with hindsight is a mug's game.

Back in early February 1994, with this rock-solid confirmation of a peak, I should have been moving massively into cash. I did sell

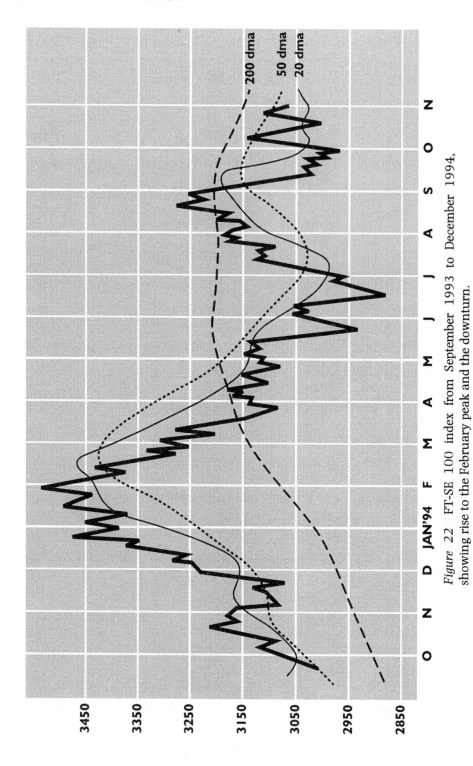

Figure 22 FT-SE 100 index from September 1993 to December 1994, showing rise to the February peak and the downturn.

around 40 per cent of my portfolio within a week of that event, but now I have seen how it unfolded, I think I would sell at least 60 per cent of my portfolio when I recognize another similar occasion. For shares in excellent small growth companies where the story continues to sound great, reducing them by a third or a half would be a sound precaution, although long-term investors should not suffer if they just ignore the downturns. One reason why I do not do this is because when I raise cash during a downturn, I can reinvest it in some of my favourite shares at much lower prices, when the tumble is mainly over.

Investors are like fisherman; they never forget the big ones that got away.

THE TEN-DAY TEST

One final indicator is extremely easy to calculate and gives an insight as to what the market might do next. This is the ten-day rolling average for the number of days out of the last ten when the FT-SE 100 index and the DJIA index have been up or down. It gets recorded for both indices as 5/5, 6/4, 7/3, etc. Since I began recording the data, there has never been a 10/0 or 0/10 record. But during the week of 3–9 August 1993, the FT-SE 100 index made five 9/1s in a row after a row of three 8/2s in late July. I know that once the market gets to 8/2, even if it stays there for a few days, it must start moving back to balance. It usually goes slowly back to 5/5 or 4/6, before it starts on another rise towards 8/2 again, or it may continue in the opposite direction, towards 2/8 on the down side.

If you decide to try my system, try to update your charts or data on a daily or weekly basis. In drifting markets, the entries can be bunched and recorded weekly. But in fast-moving markets, or when you are expecting a major turn, daily entries would keep you closer to the action. By keeping records of some of these key indicators you learn about the market's moods and you are more likely to go with the market trend, not against it. In that case, you would hopefully not be selling shares too soon in a bull market.

And you will quickly learn when it is time to protect your profits by selling.

Moreover, for the autumn and winter rise up to February 1994, there were clear signals in January of a coming top. The FT-SE 100 made three big swings within that month, dropping down to hit the 20-day moving average twice, before bouncing up strongly off it again. High volatility in the movement of a share price or index is evidence of a possible top formation.

In early February 1994 you may have ignored all these technical and fundamental factors discussed above, even though they were suggesting it was then time to sell. Yet even if you were still fully invested, all was not lost. By the end of February, on the chart, you would have spotted the formation of a dead cross, as the falling 20-day moving average fell through the falling 50-day average. And throughout March, these two averages stayed resolutely above the falling index, as all three lines moved down together. All these signals were indicating a very negative picture. Together they are helpful for making the timely sell decisions for your portfolio.

Retaining your profits in a falling market is more important than making big gains on the rise.

CHECK LISTS FOR WHEN TO BUY AND SELL

Here is a summary of the key points that help in making crucial buy and sell decisions by monitoring the main action in the market. This is important for knowing when to buy shares you have been watching, as they may start to move higher when the market begins rising strongly. If you think a bull market trend may be about to unfold, this is the time to plan your buy decisions and undertake active monitoring, so you can maximize your gains. However, you should not act too hastily, in case the market continues to drift and the big rises get deferred.

Every portfolio is almost bound to contain a few shares where you think the future prospects may not be as rosy as you had previously anticipated. It is to deal with these shares where your commitment has wilted that it helps to judge when the market is peaking, so you can sell them with your profits intact, or before small losses increase during the oncoming downturn.

WHEN TO BUY

i   A major fundamental event has switched the market mood from negative or doubtful to firmly positive; these events might include a fall in interest rates, a change of government, good news in America, a global rise in markets, tax cuts to stimulate the economy, etc.

ii The financial press start to write in a more optimistic mood.

iii Major international or national people will make confirmatory speeches outlining the main reasons for the bullish scenario.

iv On the charts:

   (a) The market has gone through a base-building or trading range phase, which can clearly be seen to be ending.
   (b) The rising 20-day moving average makes a golden cross with the 50-day moving average.
   (c) The 200-day average is flat or beginning to rise.
   (d) There is heavy volume, a large number of advancing shares, more new highs than lows.
   (e) The market may gap up strongly.
   (f) All the main FT-SE indices will be rising in unison, confirming the up-trend.
   (g) Watch for a strong up-trend channel which should shortly become apparent on the charts.

When everyone is a buyer, who is left to buy?

WHEN TO SELL

i   There may be a serious national or international event that triggers rising fear in the markets. The death of a key political figure, an outbreak of war, rising interest rates, any unexpected news item after a strong rise, which implies a market peak has been reached.

ii The financial press start to become gloomy or jittery.

iii Important people make major speeches outlining the grave nature of the crisis.

iv On the charts:

(a) There will probably have been a previous big bull market surge which is now faltering and running out of momentum.

(b) The main FT-SE 100 index is way above all its moving averages, including the longer-term, 200-day average.

(c) The index will show several days of very high volatility, with big rises followed by big falls.

(d) The numbers of shares hitting new highs or advancing each day may have reached amazing levels.

(e) There will be major down moves in the indices on heavy volume, large numbers of declining shares and large numbers of new lows on a daily basis.

(f) The falling index will cut down rapidly through the falling 20-day moving average and then through the 50-day average in two dead crosses.

(g) The falling index will stay below these two averages.

(h) The index will drop swiftly through the 20-day moving average even though this average may still be rising.

TRACKING COMPANIES

Knowing what the market is doing is crucial for protecting profits when a major turning point for a decline looks likely. A sound response to this big-picture event is a key part of your overall action plan. It becomes a specific weeding-out exercise, to release funds to hold as cash, ready to reinvest when the next big upturn looms into view. At the peak turning point, therefore, it is best to raise some cash by selling out completely those shares that have given disappointing results, while holding onto your best performers. These will become your 'core holdings', hopefully for large long-term gains.

Time spent during the downturn prospecting for new core holdings to add to your portfolio can be richly rewarded when the market has another rally up. We looked at buy and sell signals for choosing individual shares in Chapter 2, using the FASTER GAINS formula, and again in Chapter 4, when we discussed signals in the charts. These two areas provide the main source of your stock-picking routine but should always be pursued with the wider market picture in mind.

When making buy decisions check on the date for the next results announcement, either interim or final, for your selected company. If the next set of results is some way off, say two months, investors will not yet be worrying about them. But if they are less than eight weeks ahead, there may be buying in the run-up to the results. Sometimes, after a good rise in the shares, there may be profit-taking before results are announced, or directly after the announcement. If the results are bad, the share price may now drop to reflect the disappointment. All these factors need to be thought about before a buying decision is finalized. I prefer to wait for the results, to confirm that the current and future earnings and the whole growth story are both still on course. Then I can safely make a buy decision on all the new information available with the results. Waiting for this confirmation is of even greater importance for assessing the prospects of loss-making start-up companies and early recovery situations.

Better returns are achieved by concentrating your resources in just a few promising companies.

I watch both the companies I am invested in, plus the good prospects I have unearthed, which I may soon invest in. I usually try to track these prospects carefully and often make a definite investment decision, yes or no, after analysing the next set of company results as soon as they have been announced. If I still feel unsure, I wait to read opinions on them in the financial press or read the latest company report.

There are several company events to watch out for, as they give vital information on how well the company is doing. If the news is truly exciting, there will be a strong buying surge. This can be a wonderful moment, if it happens to a share you are holding. The most important company events are announcements of final and interim results, annual general meetings, and extraordinary meetings called to pass some specific piece of business, like authorizing a rights issue.

The publication of the annual report is important, as it might include details of current trading or future prospects. I keep records of X-dividend dates (on which I will only qualify for the dividend if I am holding the shares on that day), the dates for dividend payments and the amounts of dividends due. Then I can quickly check that money due to me has correctly arrived. All these major company details get logged in my page-a-day diary, or in my dealing records, where they form a handy, quick-to-find, collection.

It can be a tragedy to get panicked out of a ten-bagger company share before it has made its great surge up.

PYRAMID-BUILDING WITH SUPER STOCKS

As the story unfolds, with your profits soundly building, you might feel confident enough to add more shares to your existing position in some of your super-stocks. In the jargon this is called 'pyramiding your position'. It was another route to great profits often used by Jesse Livermore. Each month's *Chart Breakout* newsletter includes one growth or recovery story where this approach looks promising.

Choose the right moment to add; on an announcement of excellent results, or good news announced as a trading statement or the arrival of a major new contract. For safety, always check on the chart to see if there has been a new breakout on this news. The chart helps you decide on the best time to add. It will show the ending of another base-building phase, with the price breaking out on the up-side, hopefully for another upwards spurt. The charts of Telspec (Figure 3, p. 38) Coda (Figure 9, p. 78) and Filtronic Comtek (Figure 10, p. 79) show these periodic pauses. At the end of each of these, an additional investment would have proved highly profitable.

Increasing a commitment in one share needs careful monitoring to make sure it does in practice what you expected it to do. This is a key element for improving risk control. If the shares are not progressing as you thought they would, you should be ready to revise your plans as soon as you see they have gone wrong.

Monitoring keeps you in control, able to adjust if market conditions change.

Always rework your fundamental analysis price targets before adding more shares, to ensure there is plenty of up-side profit in that story. This routine, watching a share price chart for the end of a base-building pause, and reworking the fundamental figures, can be used for the 'ones that got away' which you never bought, or sold too soon.

If the profitable story is intact and the share price breaks out again after a pause, this could give you an opportunity to make a new investment. After all, many other investors will be entering the action around this time, otherwise the new breakout from the base-building phase would never occur. This is the way I managed to make such a high return on my Unipalm investment, even though I was out of the country when the first big rise occurred.

CHOOSING A BUYING PRICE

There are several points to note about following a share you are planning to buy. Start by deciding how many shares you will hold and set a price at which you hope to buy them. This may be the current price, so an instant decision has to be made. If not, keep tracking until your target buy price appears.

Learning how share prices behave relative to their short-term moving averages can help you plan an entry price, but you must check the share is not overpriced on such fundamentals as the price/earnings ratio and your target price. If your buy and target price are too close, the profits from this investment will be correspondingly small.

The best-prospect small companies are those with several years of good earnings growth ahead of them, so you can ride the earnings curve right up to the company's mature phase. Try to buy either on a clear breakout, after a phase of profit-taking, when the price has dropped back to bounce off a moving average, or after the base-building phase is complete. Tracking the share before it has reached one of these buy signals gives you the best chance to buy at your chosen price. You may have to be patient, waiting for that situation to occur. If the right moment never arrives, you may have to abandon that prospect and start tracking an alternative one.

The best sell signal is when you can't sleep at night.

WHAT WENT WRONG?

After buying a share, I often monitor it for the first month or so, to ensure it behaves as I expected. If it falls, I go back to the estimates and calculations, to see where I went wrong. Then I have to ask myself some hard questions. Did I buy too soon? Will the price recover? Are there special factors causing the price fall which do not affect the long-term performance? How far will this share price fall before I lose my nerve? I feel much happier sitting on a falling share price if I have a cushion of profits behind me, if I think I have simply run into a bout of normal profit-taking, or if I know the underlying story for the company is still very positive.

With a new investment, I set a sell price about 10 per cent below the buy price. This is my 'stop loss' limit. It is meant to do just that: to *stop me from taking a large loss* if I have got the story wrong. I often check the positions of the moving averages, before deciding to sell, in case the share is diving down to meet it, before bouncing up again and recovering. The price may fall on profit-taking, or directors' selling, or if the whole market is falling. I am much less tolerant of large price falls on small loss-making shares in companies which are hopefully 'expecting' to make superb profits in the future, but not yet. As the price falls my doubts increase and I may sell, to watch from the sidelines. With small companies, news is infrequent. You may watch in horror as the price plunges, with no idea why it happens. When you do know the reasons, it is much easier to assess a situation before you sell in haste.

ASSET-ALLOCATIONS DESIGNED FOR PROFITS

Although everyone knows it is best always to let the profits run, in practice it is sometimes easier said than done. One reason why it is such a good idea is so you can make the big gains you want, without worrying about the need to choose other shares. If the shares you have bought are performing well, then changing to other shares can in itself become an added risk since, as we have seen, every new investment has to be monitored from the outset to ensure it behaves as you expected. And if it does not, you have to bear the costs of buying and selling, plus any accompanying losses.

Try to organize the asset allocation in your portfolio so that you have the best chances of making big gains. This means never having too much money *accidentally* in any one sector. This rule can be broken if you suddenly realize that many of the shares in that section of the market are undervalued and could soon be due for a major rerating. Or there might be a big profits leap ahead for several companies in that sector, which would create the same rerating prospects. Tracking your shares is an ongoing task to keep you up to date with the ever-changing market. Ways to do this are covered in Chapter 8.

You can make a great success of investing, if you learn how to buy early and sell early.

CHAPTER 8

Fine tuning for success

To have money is good, to have control of money is still better. Leo Rosten

One of the most encouraging aspects of learning to be a do-it-yourself investor is that it can be practised by anyone, regardless of age, sex, occupation or physical condition. Nor is it necessary to become a millionaire in order to gain tremendous benefits from this new-found experience. Each person can measure his progress in his own terms and each person will feel the benefits of his growing skills in his own way. It is never a beauty contest in which there can only be one winner.

Learning to be successful with your investments is a very personal achievement. I don't believe a stranger can do this for you as well as you can do it for yourself, once you have mastered the elementary fundamental steps. Moreover, whether we accept the fact or try to ignore it, everyone has to take charge of their own financial destiny sooner or later. It can make a profound impact on your living standard if you get your money working for you as early as possible. It is impossible to describe what a powerful feeling you can obtain from mastering the skills which allow you to make money on your stock market investments. You have to do it to feel it.

> *You may know how to make a successful investment without ever being able to do it.*

In the same way that no two musicians will ever play any one piece of music identically, so everyone interprets investment expertise in a unique way, according to their own needs, personality, abilities and tolerance for risk. While the essential principles and discipline will be universally applicable, the way investment skills are practised will be exclusive to every investor. For this reason, the magpie approach, collecting little snippets of wisdom from the books you read, is an excellent way to build up your own personal expertise.

However, for every investor, whether they recognize the actual structure that underpins their efforts or not, the first priority is to focus on the three main planks of an investment programme: the strategy of what you want to achieve in terms of the time it will take and your 'real' money goal; the tactics of how you are going to achieve this target in good time; and the action plan, the step-by-step guide to ensure you stay on course to reach your chosen targets according to the plan you have devised.

HANG ON TO YOUR CAPITAL

For me, although the route has been fraught with obstacles and detours, I have broadly stayed on course with the goals I set myself in the spring of 1990. What I failed to anticipate was the irritating way unexpected difficulties would crop up constantly to move the goal posts I had erected. After I had been investing for about four years, a knowledgeable friend said people like me, who are grimly determined to make money in the markets, rarely achieve their aim. He thought this is because the harder you try to make your money grow, the more risk-taking and bloody-minded obstinacy creep into your plans to chase that one aim above all others. And these two hazards jeopardize your success. As in other areas of life, if you try too hard, success becomes increasingly elusive.

> *When you put money in the market, you often find that the 'doing' is tougher than the planning.*

Well, every rule is made to be broken in the tough world of growing wealthy. But I think I have finally worked out why I never succumbed to a speculator's urge in a devil-take-all fashion as I stayed fixated on reaching my goals. Having started to invest late in life, I was resolved to lose only the barest minimum of money. Facing any doubtful situation, I reasoned it was better to sacrifice a possible gain than to accept a large possible loss. Everyone must find their own route to protect their hard-saved cash, but my solution was to sell as soon as I felt uncomfortable with a falling share price or a company story. Panic selling is my personal investment safety valve. It may be stupid, idiotic or naïve to let it take control, but it does serve a useful purpose. It is always working *for me* to prevent me making big losses when I think I am 'out of my depth'. Behaviour that appears to be stupid is only stupid if it is irrational. Now I have a rational explanation for my bouts of panic selling, they no longer worry me. This solution may not work for more ambitious investors, but I think it could be a sensible approach, when used in moderation, for raw beginners who are genuinely petrified of losing their capital.

THE PURPOSE OF YOUR SYSTEM

Of course, if you think things through in a logical way, the chances are the investment plans you devise will bring handsome returns. By focusing on proper planning you can increase your profits and minimize your losses, because you will know what to do if things start to go wrong. You will have thought about the best opportunities for investing and so will be ready to act decisively when they emerge. You will be able to improve your understanding of the way markets work and know how to time your purchases and sales of company shares.

Reading about and planning risk control will help you to reduce the possibilities of loss. Inadequate plans increase the chances of larger losses. To have no investment scheme at all is a recipe for financial disaster. By strictly following your chosen method with all its stages, you can stay in better control of every investment situation.

The most important advice for beginners is simply to keep going, by taking one step at a time.

DEVISE A SET OF RULES

As we noted in Chapter 5, if you have a set of rules to suit your investment routine, it reduces the risk of making large losses if your plans do go wrong. You should always try to obey the rules of your own system. This enforces good self-control. Don't change your rules unless you first do a full review of your recent investment performance (say every six months, or at least once every year). You should stay flexible. Plan to run your profitable investments but cut the loss-making ones quickly. This discipline is difficult, as you may get attached to the shares you are holding, or you might feel that selling them is an admission that you timed the investment wrongly in the first place. Overcoming your own bruised ego is one of the most difficult tests for investors. No one likes to admit to mistakes, but the sooner you can accept them by analysing what went wrong, the sooner you will put yourself into a position where you are well in control.

You can count the main rules for successful investing on the fingers of two hands.

Following your chosen stock-picking routine gives you a method of carefully studying the risks to minimize the chances of losses. And if you monitor the progress of each investment both before and after you buy it, have a sell price in mind in case the share does not perform as you expected, and are willing to act decisively if that sell price is hit, your confidence will grow because a disciplined approach will almost certainly bring good gains in due course.

KNOWING YOURSELF

An important early battle is to learn to handle the 'enemy within the gates'. This means learning to understand your own investment psychology. The reason I have discussed my panic selling 'weakness' is to show that it took me the best part of five years to understand why I persisted with what I fully recognized was a ridiculous form of behaviour. It was only when I finally came to understand the psychology that drove me to go on repeating it that I knew I had, at long last, mastered the wretched thing. This does not mean I no longer panic, as I still occasionally do, when things crop up that I am not expecting. But now I accept it as part of my investment protection apparatus. I think I will be able to finally dump it when I feel financially secure, whenever that magic moment should arrive. This is the kind of reasoning that every novice investor should explore when confronted by errors, difficult situations and investment failures.

Every investor needs to examine his own investment psyche from time to time. Is it wired for winning or losing? Sometimes you might discover that *you* are the most important person preventing your portfolio from growing because you are taking rash or ill-timed decisions that do not allow your investments to prosper as they should, in spite of all your careful preparation. When I listed the 'ones that got away' it was to highlight this lurking tendency, which probably affects most beginners, of losing confidence too soon and not having sufficient patience to let the profits materialize.

REDUCE THE RISKS

All investment is based on anticipating future share price movements, hence the risk. Your research is designed to find the big movers before they make their main move; either because there is a new product, a profits surge, a takeover or a market rerating for an undervalued company. This big move may not happen, or may take years. And such delays can ruin your carefully laid schemes. You can reduce the risks considerably by assessing the probabilities. This means looking closely at the possibility of gains versus the possibilities of losses. When these two elements have been properly assessed the chances for profits will be overwhelmingly in your favour. If they are neglected, the risk of loss is much greater.

WEIGHING UP THE PROSPECTS

As cash is always limited, you must try to focus on the best prospects. You should weigh up the 'pros' and 'cons' of any share you are considering. Look for those with the greatest mileage for gain.

For comparing company prospects, some of the pointers to look for include the following:

i   Which of two shares has the best fundamentals (use FASTER GAINS)?
ii   Which of two has the best profit potential (using the target prices calculations)?
iii Which of two has the lowest risk factor, judging, for example, by the price movements on the charts?
iv   Which of two is in the best sector with the greatest possibilities for gains, perhaps because it is in a leading edge sector?
v   Which of two has the potential to grow five or ten times over, because of the strength of the story in that sector, that industry or in that company's niche products?
vi   Which of two has the best prospects of a profitable future, again, by examining the stories involved?
vii Which of two fits best with the current stage of the market?
viii Which of two offers a better future growth in dividends?

In the end, all equity valuations depend on earnings.
Fund Manager, **Investor's Chronicle**

One way I tackle the issue of comparing two prospects is to 'buy' the two shares on paper. With a sum of money, say £3,000 (ignoring the costs, which are the same for both cases), I work out the profits I would make if I bought the two promising shares I am considering. Obviously, I would only get 500 shares in Company A, if each cost 600p, disregarding expenses, and 3,000 shares at 100p in Company B. The possible profits depend on the target prices I think are achievable and what period of time it would take to reach them. This calculation does sometimes help to differentiate between two possible prospects. If company A rises to 850p in 18 months while Company B reaches 135p around the same date, the profit from A would be £1,250 and from B £1,050. Calculations like this need not be crude guesses if you have worked through the examples on future earnings streams and future price/earnings ratios as illustrated in Chapter 2.

It is wisest to try to select the lowest risk investment by evaluating the 'pros' and 'cons' of each investment choice, since you are hoping every share you choose will earn its keep. This is doubly important if you only have a modest starting capital sum. You can try to calculate the chances of being right on each share you are considering by developing a sound stock-picking routine, such as FASTER GAINS, or by checking on the chart, on the company's fundamentals and other key factors, like sector analysis. As we noted in Chapter 7, letting the profits run is another proven route to risk control as it allows the gains to pile up without having to take on additional risks by switching into another investment. By staying with a winning position, you have eliminated the problem of having to search for and find another good prospect to invest in.

Every time you buy a new share, there is the risk it will not behave as you planned.

Always try to calculate a suitable buy and sell price for each share to determine the risk involved. You can attempt to work out the size of the possible profit versus the size of the possible losses. Also, it may help if you try to visualize a 'worst-possible' scenario. This means thinking through all the key issues that could turn your imagined 'event' into a reality. If you are still happy and determined to invest in that particular share, work out a contingency plan so you can get out fast if things turn sour.

You should always take appropriate actions to try to improve your risk control. However, *planning the risk is less important than actually controlling it once an investment has been made.* At all costs, you must avoid the 'frozen rabbit' effect when a price movement against your investment is so unexpected you feel paralysed and unable to act. For the best risk control, every move should have been fully anticipated in advance! This may be the ideal to which all investors strive but it is certainly possible, and most desirable, to have a back-up plan lined up for dealing with ideas that go wrong.

The most important task is the avoidance of large losses. This is achieved by cutting losses fast through setting sell limits. Whenever you buy a share, you should immediately set a selling limit, in case things go wrong. And be prepared to stick to those sell prices if events unfold in an adverse way. At these times, while watching a price diving against you, the ability to come to a quick decision might make the difference between a modest and a massive loss.

> *If you lose all your capital in a string of poor share choices, you completely lose your chance to make up the loss.*

Other ways to improve your risk control include tracking your chosen share in the market on a daily basis to find the best possible buy price. You may have to be patient until it arrives. However, when it does, you should be willing to act decisively.

STAY ON TARGET

You should try not to get discouraged if things do not work out as you planned. The secret of success is to carry on fine tuning your portfolio, to ensure you have the greatest prospects of making profits from the few shares you are holding. In addition to the fine tuning, you must be willing to stay flexible and review your progress at regular intervals. Looking after your share portfolio is a bit like raising a family. You can't just leave it to happen successfully on its own.

> *Nothing truly worthwhile is ever very easy to achieve.*

REGULAR REVIEWS

A review of your portfolio and its performance once every month will help to keep you focused. This is especially easy if you have good and detailed records. If you have an early success, try to dissect it, to see if it is a repeatable event. Keep a record of the values of the portfolio, including the cash, so that you can judge over a six-month period if your nest egg is growing, and if so, how well it is doing in percentage terms compared to a general UK index such as the FT-SE-A All-Share index.

It makes good sense to review your progress regularly, say once every three months. Calculate the exact value of your current portfolio after three to six months, if you have made no changes, to see if any of your shares has reached your set target price. If the story still looks intact, you can revise your target price upwards and stay with that company, to watch how events unfold over a further three- to six-month period. One of my favourite games is guessing how the whole portfolio will grow if every share reaches its set target, say by 31 December. Of course, many things can change before the finish date arrives, but I am sometimes amazed at how quickly some target prices are reached if the market begins a pre-Christmas rally in December.

FACE THE PROBLEMS

However painful, it is always a good idea to attempt to analyse what went wrong if you make a large early loss. If you can list the reasons for it, you will probably save yourself a huge amount of aggravation in the future. And once you have spent time analysing what you did wrong, you will be less likely to repeat the same mistake again.

It can be a most frustrating experience to keep repeating one stupid mistake several times. I know, because there have been many occasions when I have failed to learn from my mistakes. When I have finally faced up to the stupidity of my actions, I have written myself a short note in huge block letters, reminding me of my obstinate folly. The note gets clipped to my trading compliment slips, so I see it every time I handle my records. It stares back at me every day for a month or so, reminding me of my stupidity, while I take in the message it is giving me – not to repeat it.

Mistakes are only expensive if you learn nothing from them.

FINE TUNING

Basically, you must be willing to follow the fortunes of the shares you have bought, to ensure your portfolio stays on target to hit your preset goals. Always use the buy and sell signals in your stock-picking routine, especially if they are confirmed by the charts.

Keep your initial investment modest and watch to see how it performs. If things quickly begin to go wrong, it may be best to sell and have a rethink. If you are a stoical investor type, with strong nerves, you might be willing to hang on longer, in case the story does come right, but always ensure you have set proper sell limits in case it does not. However, you should try not to confuse a firm approach with a 'macho' attitude that refuses, at all costs, to accept that your investment idea was flawed, or just very badly timed.

Improving your knowledge is one of the best ways of reducing risk. Another key way of reducing risk is to try to stay flexible. Be prepared to adjust your system to the realities of investing as you go along. I think the worst mistake most novice investors make is to have done inadequate preparation. Then, when a situation occurs that they had not expected, the most natural reaction is to wait, do nothing and see if the bad position corrects itself. In most cases, this wait-and-see approach proves more costly than taking an instant loss. A better approach is to work out what has gone wrong and make new plans on how you should proceed. This is often the harder option, but it can save money if you persuade yourself to sell a losing share earlier.

You should try to improve your system by learning quickly from your mistakes. Even the most skilful investors make mistakes. The greatest benefit from a mistake is to admit to having made it at the earliest possible moment, exit from it as quickly as possible, and learn as soon as you can exactly what went wrong. You should never be afraid to admit to mistakes and reverse a bad decision quickly.

Use your mistakes wisely and they can be a short cut to your future investment success.

PREPARE FOR HOLIDAY BREAKS

It can be most disconcerting suddenly to realize that a holiday you planned several months ago is going to coincide with a really cliff-hanging time in the market. Doing this on a regular basis has turned out to be a constant feature of my investment experience. It happened in November 1990, when I was out of Britain when Mrs Thatcher left office. It happened again in September 1992, when I was going on a cruise which had been arranged almost a year previously. In August the currency markets were in turmoil over the Exchange Rate Mechanism (ERM) and the forthcoming French referendum. We were planning to begin our holiday on 5 September. I had absolutely no idea what was going to happen, but I decided cash would be the safest place for most of our funds. Accordingly, when I left, 80 per cent of the portfolio had been cashed in, with just two or three very small growth share holdings still in place.

Even when the market is drifting, some of the small growth shares with good prospects will be rising.

We heard about the expulsion of Sterling from the ERM on 17 September, the day after it happened, as one of the passengers had a radio, but our holiday still had over a week to run. As I pointed out earlier, it is a great help to ask the newsagent to keep back copies of the daily financial paper, so you can update yourself after you return from a holiday break. I found this extremely useful in September 1992, as I was able to read all the commentaries on the Sterling fiasco and the views of the financial analysts after it had occurred. There was no doubt it had been a major bullish turning point for the UK market. With all the back issues I was soon able to devise a new investment plan, catch up with my targets, and I had reinvested my cash back into the stock market by late September.

At the time, I was still so unfamiliar with economic events, I was rather vague on what the outcome of Britain's expulsion from the ERM really meant. By reading what the commentators and brokers were saying in the few days before and after 16 September, I soon realized that this was a significant event for a new bull market. UK interest rates could now be lowered and economic recovery had been made possible for Britain, now we were no longer tied to the high interest rate regime operating in Europe. Occasionally, it helps to read up on financial analysis some time after it was written, to get a broader perspective.

Shares in very good companies bought at the peak of the market may, sadly, turn out to be poor investments.

Although I had missed the first big rise after the turn, I was soon able to put all the money back into the market. Because it was a major turning point, it was not too late to enjoy the big up-trend that developed. The FT-SE 100 index rose from 2,370 on 16 September to 3,065.5 by the year-end. This was a gain of 29 per cent in under four months. There was clearly plenty of leeway for making good gains, as the smaller shares I like to follow almost always take a little time to catch up with the main FT-SE 100 action. They often begin their rises after the blue chip shares have led the way higher.

This lag is excellent news for investors searching for little growth shares with big prospects as you can be more certain that the major turning point has occurred, when all the FT-SE 100 shares are rising, without necessarily missing the big surge in the small shares you plan to buy. Investors who focus on small growth or recovery shares have this time lag advantage, for after the main market turns, there will still be time before most of the small shares move strongly ahead.

Taking a holiday break is a good moment to review your full portfolio before leaving. If you are worried about the uncertain state of the market or possible adverse events that may occur while you are away, do not be afraid to sell your most doubtful shareholdings to raise some cash. Concentrate mainly on selling shares you feel most doubtful about. You can easily catch up with events on your return, especially if you can read up on what you have missed while you were away.

GOING STALE

Everyone has an off-period at some time, when your stock-picking ideas dry up or you find you are making more poor selections than winning ones. This is more likely to happen to me during times when the market is falling or drifting. In particular, I got very depressed during the long downturn of February 1994 to March 1995. This was my first true experience of a bear market and I found it very dispiriting. If you hit a spell like this, there are several ways to tackle it.

Beware the bears, when they are out in force; they like to give investors a hard squeeze.

First, you could try reducing your holdings down to the purely profitable growth shares, or you might consider taking a complete break for a month or two. Just find something else to do and do not look at the market at all. However, this approach may not suit you, in which case you might prefer to rethink either your outline or detailed plans, or review the phases of your action plan. If necessary, rework or revise your latest investment idea, or simply drop it and find the space for a pause. You will know when you should take a break, because your latest purchases will be showing more losses than gains.

If you feel really jaded, you might decide to go back and rethink your complete investment scheme, right from the start. Or try rereading your favourite guru books. Their advice is often a renewed source of inspiration. The ones I found most helpful are listed at the end of the book. Or you might just go through your 'bullet point' notes a few times.

The best tonic for a jaded investment performance is the arrival of a new bull market.

MANY ROUTES TO SUCCESS

Once you learn to master your own investment personality, you will find that with shrewd portfolio management, outstanding returns can be achieved by proper preparation. This usually means by concentrating your resources on just a few promising companies. Such a plan needs careful preparation to avoid sudden disasters. Try to be consistent in the time and effort you devote to your portfolio. Never behave like the crazy motorway drivers who rush up behind you, furious to overtake, and then dawdle infuriatingly in front of you once they are ahead. A consistent but focused pace will improve your results as you work steadily towards making your financial dreams come true.

If you decide you prefer holding a larger range of shares, with a smaller amount invested in each, then this needs even more careful monitoring, as the wider the range of shares you hold, the greater is the chance that one or two may seriously disappoint you. And if a few are really profitable, the small amount you have invested in them means they will not pull the performance of the whole portfolio up to compensate for the poor choices. Yet again, however, excellent results are possible if the whole portfolio has been carefully chosen with a good stock-picking routine, if continuous monitoring is applied and, above all, if you are prepared to be both patient and alert.

I was amazed to read in May 1996 that large numbers of TESSAs (Tax Exempt Special Savings Accounts) which matured, after a five-year savings period, in the first few months of 1996 had been left on deposit without the owners reinvesting the proceeds into new TESSAs. It seems astonishing that people who are saving money in special tax-free deposit accounts should not trouble to update their plans when they mature. This laxity is either due to forgetfulness or a sudden surge in wealth that has made monitoring the TESSAs less acute.

Whatever the reasoning behind this lack of attention to maturing TESSAs, monitoring the performance of your investments need not be such tedious work, even though it might sound like it. Investing for financial security is a very personal thing. Everyone will tackle it in their own unique way. Many investors might decide to settle on a portfolio of unit trusts and just keep adding to these to build up a sizeable nest-egg as one year follows the next. Others might choose a selection of major blue chip companies and hold them for years without worrying over short-term fluctuations. These investment approaches naturally demand very minimal monitoring. I am in a hurry to build up my capital to a level at which I feel financially secure. Then I too will join these laid-back long-term investors and concentrate on other leisure activities. But until I reach that happy state, regular monitoring is another aspect of risk control. It means I stay alert to the dangers of unexpected changes which would prompt me to sell a share because its performance has suddenly begun to falter, or where the company story has changed for the worst.

For novice investors who want to monitor their progress routinely, as I do, the efforts should prove rewarding because the closer the attention you pay to your shareholdings, the better the ultimate performance should be. Finally, then, we need to summarize all this welter of information to get the main line of priorities into focus. This topic is covered in Chapter 9.

When it comes to making big profits, the person who is working hardest against you may be yourself.

The plan in action

The first step on a journey is the longest.

Having arrived at this last chapter, novice investors might still be wondering how they should knuckle down and get their financial act together. This chapter is a short resumé of the main ideas in the book, to bring all the strands together.

THE STARTING POINT

Small investors who already have some experience of the markets will probably use my magpie approach, focusing on those items which seem most attractive to them personally. I still do this whenever I read another book on the topic. These little nuggets that I take from my reading get slotted into the routines I usually follow, to help my investment system to work more smoothly, or hopefully, to give me better results. For outright beginners with full-time jobs, I feel sure that a 'slowly-as-you-go' approach is the best way forward. It is clearly a wonderful boon in these uncertain times for those fortunate enough to have full-time employment. But it is all too easy to become complacent and spend most of your life working for your money instead of making at least some of your hard-earned cash work for you.

Money is only important to those who have very little.

Everyone should undertake a regular yearly 'wealth check', to ensure that the three prongs of your long-term plans are in place. Even in retirement, which on present forecasts can easily take us from our sixties into the late-eighties, we need to know what our financial strategies are, how we are going to achieve them and what we should do if a routine wealth check reveals a nasty shortfall between what we hope to achieve and what looks possible on present plans. Everyone should tackle at least some of the essential reading, to keep informed on the latest financial scene. This means taking more than a cursory glance at the money pages of the Saturday or Sunday papers before passing rapidly on to the sports or review sections. I am sure that money-watching is only a bore to people who have never enjoyed the excitement of watching financial decisions they have taken for themselves reap a rich reward.

MAKING PROGRESS

Further reading and paper trials are the next step on the route to building confidence in your ability to handle your own money matters more efficiently. You can then begin exploring the huge range of available collective investments, unit and investment trusts, from the helpful Saturday and Sunday financial press, which allocates a great deal of space to this important topic on a regular basis. Perhaps there is an investment club operating in your area which would cut down the amount of time, effort and money you have to spend to get your plans up and running. Maybe you could sound out the idea of starting a club with colleagues at work, or with neighbours or friends. You can begin to build the simple files I recommended in Chapter 3 and start routinely tracking the market as indicated in Chapter 7, to build up your knowledge of the 'wider picture'. As pointed out earlier, simply learning to avoid investing at the peak when optimism is at its highest, will boost the performance of your savings, even if you decide to do nothing more active than that.

The opportunities are out there just waiting to be recognized.

START BUYING SHARES

Finally, when you have reached the stage where you have built up a portfolio of unit trusts that are actually showing a profit; when you have learned a great deal more than you first knew about the markets and your own attitudes to investing; and when you feel confident enough to take the plunge, you may decide the time is right to begin buying shares in publicly quoted companies. Therefore, as a final refresher, I am including a few of my 1996 investment decisions to bring the whole important topic of stock-picking into focus.

As a warning I would like to point out that the shares I bought or considered buying in the early months of 1996 are *examples only* of how my stock-picking routine works in practice. By the time this book is published, the prices and future prospects of the companies discussed below could be very different; the outlook for the market may have completely changed; or better potential purchases may have emerged using the routines I am about to outline. The discussion below is intended for guidance only.

To make a success of your investments, always use the clues that market action provides.

MY SINGLE COMPANY PEP SAGA

After selling my shares in Unipalm in 1995 there was almost £6,000 in my Single Company PEP which had started out as

£3,000 during 1994. I wanted to go on building it up by selecting a small growth share with the potential to double the size of the fund within two to three years. However, I was not immediately sure which share was going to give me this result. One disadvantage of Single Company PEPs is that cash can only sit in the PEP for a maximum of 42 days before it *must* be reinvested, and it all has to be invested in just one company. I find these constraints very irritating, especially as I now had a fund of £6,000 to put into one share.

I had a couple of false runs in the autumn of 1995, buying and selling two technology shares within a few months. The first of these was MAID, the online information provider which had negotiated some promising contracts with big computer companies, including Microsoft. But when MAID arranged to float some of its shares on the American Nasdaq Composite index, the share price became uncomfortably volatile and I decided to sell my holding. My second choice was Azlan, a small computer network components distributor. Azlan was a recovery situation with excellent growth prospects but again, after a short period, I felt uncomfortable with it as a long-term hold. I bought Azlan at 467p on 26 October 1995, and by the time it had produced its excellent final results in early June 1996 the share price had risen to 720p. If I had been confident enough to hold on, this investment would by June have been worth £9,497 in the PEP.

> *Don't fret over a share you feel uncomfortable about.*
> *Make a decision and eliminate the 'fret'.*

In January 1996 I tried again. Including a small profit on Azlan there was now £6,380 in the PEP. On 6 January the *Techinvest* newsletter arrived, and on the strength of the write-up I decided to investigate Sage Group as a suitable long-term candidate for the PEP, using my FASTER GAINS formula.

FASTER GAINS FOR SAGE

F: Fundamental Facts on Sage reveal a solid record of unbroken growth in profits spanning ten years to the year ending 30

September 1995. Boosted by acquisitions, the company had grown its turnover from £2.1 million in 1986 to £102.2 million by 1995, a compound growth rate of 54 per cent. Sage has achieved a dominant position in the PC accounting software market in the UK and is aiming to repeat this performance in France where it has acquired three companies. The first, Ciel, was bought in October 1992, followed in 1994 by the big acquisition of SAARI for £19.1 million, and finally by the acquisition of Sybel Informatique in November 1995 for £16 million, thus completing the foundations for its French business. Future plans include expansion into the fragmented German market and the lucrative US market. Sage was floated in December 1989 and has produced an unbroken run of growth in turnover, profits and earnings per share over this ten-year period. On 23 October 1995, there was a five-for-one share split taking the shares from 1,390p to 278p each.

A: Final results for Sage in December 1995 showed the early benefits of its French acquisitions to its trading performance. **Annual earnings per share** were 53 per cent up at 13.88p from 1994's 9.08p. Sage achieves a 35 per cent margin on its UK business and it aims to achieve the same outcome in France. In December 1995, it reported that SAARI had currently lifted margins from 7 to 11 per cent with Ciel up to 17 per cent; so further improvements should be possible. On conservative growth estimates, earnings per share for 1996 could be 19p and for 1997, 24p. At a prospective price/earnings ratio of 25, which is not excessive for a company with such a strong growth record, a 1996 target price of 475p (19 × 25 = 475) looked possible with a price of 600p (24 × 25 = 600) achievable by 1997. If these forecasts work out as planned, the PEP value will be £10,896 (1,816 × 600p) by 1997 (giving a growth of 71 per cent from January 1996).

S: The Supply/Demand factors for Sage are not especially helpful as, according to *Company REFS*, the directors together held about 20 per cent of the 107 million ordinary shares, while institutional investors held approximately 11.4 per cent, leaving a large pool of over 68 per cent as freely tradeable shares.

The law of supply and demand is more important than all the analysts' opinions on Wall Street.   William O'Neil

T: For the Technical Analysis picture Sage had risen from 250p to about 345p prior to reporting its full-year results in December. This was at a new all-time high for the shares, equivalent to 1,725p before the October five-for-one share split. Early in December, the two shorter moving averages (20- and 50-day) had come very close together and had met up with the price line at 275p. This is a very bullish formation as it means all the random share price movements have been temporarily eclipsed. An upwards move from here would be positive, so when it emerged (as shown in Figure 23) I felt encouraged that the picture would continue to prove promising.

To become a successful long-term investor you have to know how to pick good shares with excellent prospects.

E: Efficient Management. The directors still hold 20 per cent of the company and so have a big incentive to continue making it successful.

R: Rich in Cash for Sage was not applicable because the company had a net debt position of £12 million in December 1995, to pay for its French acquisitions. However, the company is extremely cash-generative as it has been able to convert one-off purchasers of its accounting software packages into repeat-order customers by selling them high-margin upgrades, add-on packages, training and other useful additions. In the *Investors Chronicle* of 8 December 1995, where the preliminary full-year results were analysed, the magazine quoted that in 1995 Sage had earned £9 million in the UK from providing a telephone helpline to UK users of its products. The margins on this service alone were estimated to be not far short of 50 per cent.

G: Growth in EPS since 1990 showed a rise from 3.72p to 13.88p, a rise of 273 per cent. Over a full ten-year period, the rise was from 0.52 to 13.88p, or 2,569 per cent.

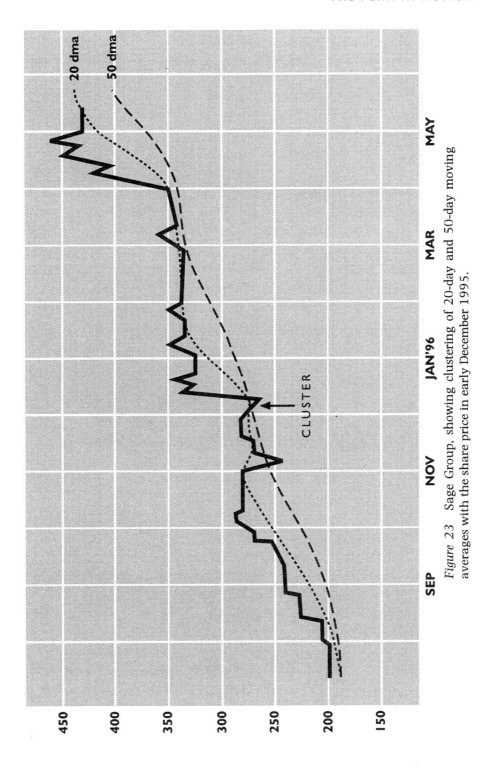

Figure 23 Sage Group, showing clustering of 20-day and 50-day moving averages with the share price in early December 1995.

A: **Active Monitoring** is still essential for every company, even for one like Sage with a superb ten-year record. However, I felt that it might possibly need less monitoring than Azlan or Maid, which is why I finally settled on Sage for the PEP.

Even if you're on the right track, you'll get run over if you just sit there. Will Rogers

I: **Institutional Support** at around 11.4 per cent is not especially strong but then I am optimistic that further years of growth will encourage more institutions to buy shares. This additional buying should help to improve the share price. The company has made significant moves into America and is operating its US acquisitions from a site in Dallas and another near Boston. If the Americans become enthusiastic about the shares, Sage's rating could rise from a prospective price/earnings multiple of 25 to around 30, giving a 1997 share price target of 720p (24p × 30 = 720). Successful American technology companies are more highly rated than their British counterparts.

N: **Something New** for Sage is the focus it is now making on expansion into Europe and America to repeat the astonishing UK success in other countries. I feel confident the long-term story will show the company is well up to repeating its proven UK performance in other locations.

S: **Stock Market Direction.** Although the market had risen well from March 1995 to January 1996, analysts were not expecting an end to the good run. I felt a purchase of Sage shares now would prove to be a good long-term investment.

I bought 1,816 Sage Group shares on 9 January 1996 at 347p. On 12 January, Chairman A.D. Goldman sold one million shares at 326p because he was planning to take a less active role in the company, although he still held 5.25 million shares. However, the news of his sale knocked the share price down to around 335p. I decided not to fret over this stroke of ill-timing and carried on hoping my investment would prove a sound long-term choice.

By June 1996, after the announcement of excellent half-year results, Sage had risen to 476p (the figure I had calculated as a target for 1996) and the value of the holding was £8,644. This is well below the value my PEP would have achieved if I had stayed with Azlan, but, surprisingly, I am not dismayed. Being right on Azlan has helped to raise my stock-picking confidence for the future, which is a bonus. Sage's half-year figures to 31 March 1996 showed earnings per share growing by 33 per cent over the same period in 1995. The three French businesses had operating margins of 18.6 per cent, three per cent up on last year, but offering plenty of scope for even more improvements. Although the investment had not so far given the growth I would have achieved if I had stayed with Azlan, it had grown by £2,265 in five months and shown a percentage rise of 35.5. This illustrates the key objective I am trying to achieve by building up my PEPs with small growth shares which should give larger capital gains than shares that are paying out higher dividends than Sage.

Researching Sage using the FASTER GAINS formula encouraged me in my belief that it could continue its unbroken record of growth, and I am happy to stay with it for the foreseeable future. However, I know I shall have to stay alert for unexpected upsets just in case the growth story runs out of steam.

No rules are written in concrete in the world of investing.
Staying flexible allows you to benefit quickly when
the mood of the market changes.

LESS INFORMATION WITH NEW ISSUES

A second story I was alerted to by an article in the *Financial Times* and one in the March 1996 issue of *Techinvest*, was F.I Group. This small information technology services company was being floated on the stock market by a placing. This means institutional investors agree to buy all the shares the company is offering to the public and small private investors cannot normally apply. One reason that the company was arousing a great deal of interest was the fact that four of its five board members are female, including chief executive Hilary Cropper, appointed in 1987. The workforce holds 54 per cent of the equity to ensure a high level of employee loyalty in what is essentially a 'people-dominated' business.

F.I is another company with a splendid profits record. For the year ending 30 April 1995, turnover was £61.7 million and pre-tax profits were £3.3 million. In the following six months revenues rose by 32 per cent (on a year-on-year basis) whilst profit before tax rose by 38 per cent to £2.09 million. The main focus of F.I's business is in stand-alone applications management. This accounts for 73 per cent of revenues, and covers ongoing support, maintenance and development of a customer's existing software applications. This market is estimated to be growing by around 37 per cent annually. F.I concentrates primarily on long-term con-tracts with large, blue chip customers in the services, retail/leisure and finance sectors of the market. The group was estimated to have a value of £60 million on its flotation.

The press coverage of F.I sounded extremely positive. I did not have any prospectus details to work with as these are not freely available to private investors if there is to be a select placing. But I liked the sound of the company and when I knew it was being placed at 235p, I decided to put it on my *Market Eye* screen on the first day of trading to watch events. However, by the time the first dealings were due to start on 10 April, sentiment in the market was looking very optimistic. When the share price opened at 285–290p I thought it was looking rather expensive as it had opened at an immediate premium of 22 per cent to the placing price of 235p. However, on the write-ups I had read and the mood in the market, I decided to buy 2,000 shares. I was able to get these at 293p at 8.32a.m. as first dealings in new issues always begin at 8.30a.m.

Although F.I finished its first day of trading at 300p, and my holding was just in profit, as it had cost me an average of 297p after commission and stamp duty, I confess I thought I had paid too high a price for my holding. However, this sector of the market is highly rated and has sound long-term growth prospects. The market went on to hit an all-time high on the FT-SE 100 index on 19 April and by the end of the month F.I's share price was hovering around 330p.

During the next two months, although the FT-SE 100 index fell off from its peak, some sections of the market continued to be strong and by early June the price of F.I shares was standing at 378p to show a gain of 27 per cent in two months. The price had risen as high as 413p at one stage, but I feel happy to hold it for the long term, to allow the growth story to unfold.

From this account, you can see that I was not able to do a FASTER GAINS check on F.I because I did not have a prospectus. I relied instead upon the press reports of its good growth history before the flotation, the excellent future prospects for the sector, the large holding of shares by the workforce which meant fewer free shares for the rest of us to compete for in the open market, and the very positive direction of the stock market at the time of the flotation.

The way to be safe is never to feel secure.

During March, I began to feel rather negative about the continuing high levels of the indices for the UK market, but in April, despite the market's mood turning quite positive again, I still felt that a downward slide might soon emerge. I decided to sell a holding of Coda, another specialist accountancy software provider, because I felt that my portfolio contained too many technology shares and I wanted to hold more cash. I reworked the estimates for Coda based on its 1997 prospects for earnings per share of 8.5p. At its current price of 240p it gave a price/earnings ratio of 28 for the next 18 months. I thought this left no room for improvement for some time, and although I still liked the company, I sold 1,500 Coda shares early in June but continue to watch it on my *Market Eye* screen. Subsequently, Coda issued a profits warning and the share price plunged to 140p – a full 100p below the price I sold at. This is a cautionary tale of woe on small, risky shares for novice investors.

Most small investors buy when they should be selling and sell when they should be buying. This is not a successful investment formula.

A CHANCE TO PYRAMID MY BRITISH AEROSPACE HOLDING

On Thursday, 6 June, while I was busy writing, I suddenly noticed British Aerospace rising on my *Market Eye* screen. The price had shot up from 888p–894p overnight to 907p–912p. This was an all-time high for British Aerospace and I thought the share would now stage a breakout. I was already holding 913 shares in British Aerospace, 900 of which were bought in September 1995 at an average cost of 695p. I took both the September 1995 interim dividend in the form of six extra shares and the March 1996 final dividend as an extra seven shares. Opting to take shares instead of a cash dividend is an excellent way of increasing a holding you are happy with as a long-term investment. It would be impossible to buy six or seven British Aerospace shares in the open market because the value of these few shares would incur very high costs. When the share price begins to rise above the price at which the company initially calculated the value of the dividend in terms of shares (say 850p for British Aerospace), the new shares will begin to show a handsome profit which would have been lost if the cash dividend had been the preferred option.

I stopped writing on that June afternoon to check out the latest position of British Aerospace in the *Company REFS*. When there is no time to do a complete FASTER GAINS, most of the crucial information I rely on can be quickly gleaned from searching out the company profile given in *Company REFS*. Estimated earnings for 1996 were 64.2p, with 79.6p for 1997. At a price of 910p for the 1997 figures, British Aerospace had a prospective price/earnings ratio of 11.4. Growth was estimated to be 28.6 per cent in *Company REFS*, indicating that there was room for a rerating on the share price, to bring the prospective price/earnings ratio up to around 14. Multiplying the 1997 estimated EPS figure of 79.6p by a prospective price/earnings of 14 gives a target price of 1,114p. This was a healthy 204p above its current price and a forecast gain of 22 per cent.

In spite of the new breakout on the share price and the relatively low rating for the share, I decided not to increase my holding but to watch how events developed. My caution was due to the fact that I was still wary of a big slide in share prices over the summer months. On Friday, 7 June, British Aerospace continued to forge ahead, as the strong breakout of the previous day indicated it might. It was one of just a handful of shares that made progress on that day, closing at 937p, while the FT-SE 100 index fell 53.5

points in a sudden fit of anxiety over a possible rise in interest rates in America.

Buy the company, not the market.

I have noticed in the past that British Aerospace is a company that responds quickly to positive news items and often moves sluggishly within a narrow range while awaiting further news on its prospects. On this June occasion, two news items had set the British Aerospace share price alight. The first was the announcement of a link up with Boeing of the US, to compete for a Ministry of Defence order worth £22 million; and the second item was a revival of talk about a stock market flotation for the European Airbus consortium, in which British Aerospace has a 20 per cent holding. This may not materialize quickly, however, because there are three other partners, Daimler-Benz Aerospace of Germany, Construcciones Aeronauticas SA of Spain and Aérospaciale of France, the latter still being a state-owned company.

Any agreement between the four partners is likely to take many months to hammer out, although the competition in the market-place for aircraft should focus their attention on the need to resolve this matter with great urgency. When I read the Stock Market Report in the *Financial Times* on Saturday 8 June, I was delighted to see that the big surge in British Aerospace had occurred on the strength of broker recommendations. ABN Amro Hoare Govett and Merrill Lynch were both reiterating their buy recommendations. Merrill Lynch had placed a valuation of 1,250p on its core defence and Airbus interests, plus 150p per share for all the rest (which includes its 20 per cent holding in the recently floated mobile telecoms company, Orange).

Success in investing is not really a game of chance like roulette: it depends crucially on preparation.

British Aerospace is an excellent example of a classic recovery share. It went through a very traumatic period in the late 1980s and its share price languished at a little over 100p during the autumn of 1992, when many analysts and observers thought the company might go bankrupt. It has taken more of the vital measures needed to improve its performance and profitability than the other members of the Airbus consortium. However, if the four partners could agree to the formation of one single company which was floated off on stock markets, British Aerospace's 20 per cent holding would immediately acquire a commercial value as brokers calculate a £4 billion-plus value for Airbus as a separate company.

PROFITS AS A CONFIDENCE-BUILDER

From March 1995 to June 1996, the major stock markets of the world, including Britain, had enjoyed a wonderful rise. It is impossible to know how long such a prolonged growth spell might continue, but it certainly worked wonders on the value of my share portfolio, as I am sure will have been the case for thousands of other small private investors. Watching the money grow is one of the greatest confidence boosters I know. I have learned to be more patient and less panicky as a result of this continuing positive environment for holding shares. There is bound to be a pause in the upward march, if not a downward slide, perhaps in the near future. But over the longer term, I feel confident that ferreting out small growth shares or good recovery stories will continue to provide opportunities for making handsome profits for those who are willing to search them out.

Unfortunately small investors often hope when they should fear, and fear when they should hope.

MAKING IT HAPPEN

Small private investors have many advantages that professionals do not have. I remember one freezing winter morning in 1995, watching a neighbour de-icing his windscreen at 8 o'clock in the morning so he could drive to work. I felt a hugely smug sensation as I turned on my *Market Eye*, knowing I can work as and when I care to, in the comfort and warmth of my own office. And during a bull market, when optimism is high, if I take a day off to meet friends, go into town or do some shopping, I always feel excited by the idea that while I am off enjoying myself, my money is still working for me and the portfolio is growing. I remain firmly convinced that any do-it-yourself armchair investor who wants to make a success of his investments can do just that. If I can do it, rest assured, anyone can. And the thrill of getting it right and watching your nest-egg grow before your eyes from the comfort of your own home really does take an awful lot of beating.

He who doesn't take risks doesn't drink champagne.

Glossary

Analysts: Professionals who work for the big brokerage and merchant banking houses analysing and reporting on national economies, individual companies and various sectors of a stock market.

Bear and bull markets: A bear market is one where prices are falling usually across the whole market for a prolonged period of weeks, months or even years. A bull market is one with a rising trend. Investors who think the market is about to fall are bearish while those who think the market will rise are bullish.

Bills and bonds: A bill is a short-term fixed interest loan stock, often issued by governments or very large corporations. UK Treasury Bills have a life of three months. A bond is any longer term fixed interest loan which guarantees to repay the capital at an agreed future date. UK Government bonds are known as Gilts and come in several time periods: short (under five years to maturity), medium (between five and fifteen years) and long (which mature after fifteen years).

Brokers: Brokers are professionals who buy and sell shares on behalf of their clients. Private individuals and institutions are not allowed to deal in shares directly with the market-makers who set the prices. Brokers act as middlemen between buyers and sellers.

Capital Gains: The increase in the capital value of investments. They are subject to a complicated form of government taxation, except for gilts which are free of Capital Gains Tax to make them more attractive.

Credit: Credit is given by banks when they advance loans to their customers, and businesses when they allow their customers to take goods and defer payment for them.

Derivatives: Derivatives are types of investment that derive their value from other types of investment; for example, an option to buy or sell a share at a future date derives from the underlying value of that share in the market at the time when the option contract is agreed.

Dividend: This is the proportion of a company's profits which is paid out to its shareholders. It is paid out twice yearly: as an interim and a final dividend.

Economic Business Cycle: This is a round of economic events that proceed in an irregular-succession.

Equities: These are freely traded stocks and shares in publicly quoted companies that do not carry a fixed rate of interest. Instead, they entitle their holders to a share in the growth of the company through an annual dividend payment.

Flotation: A flotation is a new issue of shares available to the public that occurs when a private company comes to the market and sells a percentage of its shares. A placing is offered on a selective basis: an intermediary offer is a placing with financial intermediaries who then sell the shares on to the public; or an offer for sale is made to the public and to investing institutions.

FT-SE 100 index: Monitors the performance of the top 100 publicly quoted shares by market capitalization (market value) on the UK stock market. It is weighted to take account of the largest and smallest sized companies within the hundred. It is updated throughout the day.

FT-SE Mid 250 index: This index works in a similar way. It monitors the performance of 250 medium-sized companies that together comprise this index.

FT-SE 350 index: This index covers the performance of the

FT-SE 100 and FT-SE Mid 250 shares. All three indices are updated continuously throughout the working day.

FT-SE SmallCap index: This is an index that covers a range of the small companies traded on the UK stock market.

FT-SE-A All-Share index: Covers about 900 shares on the UK market. It is updated at the start of every working day.

Futures Contract: This is a standardized stock exchange contract committing the person to buy (or sell) a specific commodity (share or index) as the representation of a basket of shares on a specified future date.

GDP: Gross Domestic Product: the amount of goods and services produced by a country in one calendar year.

Gilt Edged Bonds: British government loans which carry a fixed interest.

Gross: For investors, it means before deduction of income tax.

UK Growth and Income Trusts: Forms of unit trust which invest in companies quoted on the London Stock Exchange. They give investors exposure to either a high rate of growth or a high annual dividend payment.

Index: A selected list of publicly quoted shares which represent all others of that type.

Pensions: A savings scheme whereby a regular contribution creates a fund which from a specified date will return an income to the saver. Bear in mind that although contributions are generally tax exempt, tax will have to be paid on the eventual income derived from the fund.

PEPs: Personal Equity Plans: a government sponsored scheme for currently investing up to £9,000 each year with all income and gains free of tax. The £9,000 is split into £6,000 for a general PEP which can be invested in mainly UK-based unit or investment trusts or directly into UK publicly quoted shares; and £3,000 which must be invested in a single company PEP in which you can hold the shares of only one UK company at a time. The regulations and amounts eligible for investment can vary according to government legislation.

Put: An option to sell shares, bonds or commodities at a stated price at some future date.

Recovery Shares: These are the shares of companies that are expected to recover to a higher rating by the market. They include several types of company: those in cyclical sectors which will expand profitably as the economy recovers from a recession; good companies that have hit a problem or failed to meet investors' expectations; and companies that are plagued by problems and may recover or may go bankrupt.

Relative Strength: The ratio of the share price to the market index. It is a measure of the performance of a share relative to that market as a whole.

Reversal Patterns: Patterns in price charts which indicate that a major trend may be about to change, e.g. 'double tops' or 'head and shoulders'.

Risk: This word has various interpretations. Broadly, it is the amount which an investor stands to lose from any investment.

Shell Company: A dormant company whose value lies in its stock market quotation. It can be bought relatively cheaply and then used to raise equity finance instead of going through the more expensive process of setting up a totally new company.

Stock Market: The market for equities, or 'shares', in public companies. A buyer is actually purchasing a share in the ownership of a company.

TESSAs: Tax Exempt Special Savings Accounts: a government sponsored scheme for investing up to a total of £9,000 over a period of five years with interest free of tax.

Traded Options: An option is the right to buy or sell a share at a stated price at some future date. In recent years the market in buying or selling the options themselves has developed, and these are known as traded options.

Unit Trusts: A form of investment where investors' money is pooled in order to purchase a range of shares to spread the risk. This enables an investor to have exposure to a larger number of companies than individual resources alone might allow.

Yield: The annual rate of return on a share at the current market price.

APPENDIX II

Suggested Reading

The first group of books provides a gentle introduction to the broad topic of investing in general. It covers a wide range of views and investment approaches. The novice investor can tackle any or all of these as an introduction. They are listed in alphabetical order for easy access, but there is no special preferred reading order.

The Beardstown Ladies. *The Beardstown Ladies Common-Sense Investment Guide.* New York: Hyperion, 1994.

Blakey, George, G. *The Post-War History of the London Stock Exchange 1945–1992.* Mercury, 1993.

Drury, Tony. *Investment Clubs. The Low-Risk Way to Stockmarket Profits.* Leighton Buzzard: Rushmere Wynne, 1995.

Lefevre, Edwin. *Reminiscences of a Stock Operator.* Chicester: John Wiley & Sons, 1993.

Rogers, Jim. *Investment Biker. Around the World With Jim Rogers.* Chicester: John Wiley & Sons, 1995.

Schwager, Jack D. *Market Wizards.* New York: Harper & Row, 1990.

Every investor needs at least one 'guide book' which explains all the jargon of investing in simple terms. This book serves as an ideal reference for all the complicated terms investing contains. It can be acquired after some of the introductory books have been read. There are two excellent books here, both of which I find invaluable. These are:

Gray, Bernard. *Investors Chronicle Beginners Guide to Investment.* London: Business Books Ltd, 1991.

Slater, Jim. *Investment Made Easy: How to Make More of your Money.* London: Orion, 1994.

The list below includes another wide range of books for people who have already acquired some knowledge of or have direct investment experience. Most of these books deal in much greater depth with the various aspects of investing, especially the stock-picking routines, managing a portfolio and learning about the markets in general.

Hagstrom, Robert G. Jnr. *The Warren Buffett Way.* New York: John Wiley & Sons, 1994.

Linton, David. *Profit From Your PC. How to use a personal computer to buy and sell shares.* Leighton Buzzard: Rushmere Wynne, 1995.

Lynch, Peter. *One Up On Wall Street.* New York: Simon & Schuster, 1989.

Lynch, Peter. *Beating the Street.* New York: Simon & Schuster, 1993.

O'Neil, William J. *How To Make Money In Stocks. A Winning System in Good Times or Bad.* New York: McGraw-Hill Inc., 1988.

Schwartz, David. *1996 Schwartz Stock Market Handbook.* Burleigh Publishing Co., 1996.

Slater, Jim. *The Zulu Principle. Making Extraordinary Profits from Ordinary Shares.* London: Orion, 1992.

Slater, Jim. *PEP Up Your Wealth. How to Save Tax and Make Your Money Grow.* London: Orion, 1994.

Slater, Jim. *Beyond the Zulu Principle: Extraordinary Profits from Growth Shares.* London: Orion, 1996

Vintcent, Charles. *The Investor's Guide. Be Your Own Stockbroker. The Secrets of Managing Your Own Investments.* London: Pitman Publishing, 1995.

Weinstein, Stan. *Stan Weinstein's Secrets for Profiting in Bull and Bear Markets.* Burr Ridge: Dow Jones-Irwin, 1988.

THE INVESTORS' TOOLKIT

Analyst, 5–9 Sun Street, London EC2B 2GU.

Company REFS (Really Essential Financial Statistics), Hemmington Scott Publishing Ltd, City Innovation Centre, 26031 Whiskin Street, London EC1R 0BP.

Equity Focus, Reuters Ltd, 85 Fleet Street, London EC4P 4AJ.

The Estimate Directory, Edinburgh Financial Publishing Ltd, 1 Rothesey Terrace, Edinburgh EH3 7UP.

Financial Times, Number One Southwark Bridge, London SE1 9HL.

The Inside Track, 16 Randolph Crescent, Edinburgh EH3 7TT.

Investors Chronicle, Greystoke Place, Fetter Lane, London EC4 1ND.

Market Eye, ICV Ltd, 23 College Hill, Cannon Street, London EC4R 2RA.

The Mail on Sunday, Northcliffe House, 2 Derry Street, London W8 5TS

Money Observer, Garrard House, 2/6 Homesdale Road, Bromley BR2 9W2.

Portfolio Control (software package), City Deal Services, 9–11 St Edwards Way, Romford, Essex RM1 4PE.

Quantum Leap Stockmarket Letter and *Chart Breakout*, both by Quentin Lumsden, PO Box 1638, London W8 4QR.

Sharewatch, Equitylink Ltd, 75 High Street, Chislehurst, Kent BR7 5AG.

Stockmarket Solutions, Analyst plc, 5–9 Sun Street, London EC2M 2PS.

Synergy Software, Britannic House, 20 Dunstable Road, Luton LU1 1ED.

Techinvest, 31 Upper Mount Street, Dublin 2, Ireland.

Index